DIVORCE

AMONG THE

GULLS

An Uncommon Look
at Human Nature

William Jordan

1991

NORTH POINT PRESS

San Francisco

Some of these essays originally appeared
in the *Los Angeles Times Magazine*,
Smithsonian, and *Wigwag*.

LIBRARY OF CONGRESS
CATALOGING-IN-PUBLICATION DATA
Jordan, William, 1944–
Divorce among the gulls : an uncommon look at
human nature / by William Jordan.
    p.   cm.
ISBN 0-86547-426-5
  1. Animal behavior.   2. Animal psychology.
  3. Psychology, Comparative.   I. Title.
QL751.J66   1991
591.5′1—dc20   90-39321

For Mother, Dad, Van;
Darwin my intellectual mentor
and Darwin my beloved cat.

CONTENTS

Acknowledgments *ix*

Part I
Why the Mockingbird Sings 5
The Tender Macho Medfly Male 11
Gorilla Mums 17
In the Realm of the Roof Rat 32
Dracula Stumbles into Bed 39
Divorce Among the Gulls 56
Membership in the Pigeon Club 62
New Eden, City of Beasts 70
Cockroach Memoirs 101

Part II
Alfalfa Communion 129
The Strange Case of the Electric Ray 143
Distracting the Snake 154
Making a Dinosaur Work 171
Pictures at a Scientific Exhibition 187

ACKNOWLEDGMENTS

To those *sine quibus non*—without whom there would be no *Divorce Among the Gulls*: Judith Hand and her insights into gull behavior; Dick Bray and his tales of electric rays; Ken Konishiro, student of fruit flies; Thaya Dubois, student of and spiritual guardian to the gorillas of the Los Angeles Zoo; my friend Robyn Shirley, who patiently endures my readings over the phone; Vaughn Shoemaker, for his kind reminders on physiology; George Callison, expert on and advocate of small dinosaurs; Chris Mays and the staff of Dinamation, experts on and advocates of mechanical dinosaurs; Ellen Perry Berkeley, student and champion of feral cats; Freda Fox, student of mockingbirds who corroborated my speculations; Tony Recht, expert on the life of roof rats; Roger Carpenter, student of fruit bats and scientist who has seen the brighter light; Jerry Dragoo, disciple of skunks; Jeffrey Froke, student of Los Angeles parrots; Carolee Caffrey, student of southern California golf course crows; Bill Wirtz, former student of coyotes; Ron Knight, student of the Argentine ant; and to the staff of the Los Angeles County Museum of Natural History, students all, of creatures—Sarah George, mammals, Robert Bezy, reptiles, Charles Hogue and Roy Snelling, insects and spiders, Kimball Garrett, birds. And to those whom I have inevitably and inexcusably overlooked. My grateful, grateful acknowledgment.

DIVORCE
AMONG THE
GULLS

PART I

WHY
THE
MOCKINGBIRD
SINGS

I was lying there in the October dawn, the mind drifting toward conscious thought, the sounds of life tinkling far away in reality, a bird yodelling in the backyard shrubs, when the first thought of the day came through: The mockingbirds had gone back to regular work hours—they had abandoned the night shift. This fit with a theory I had been puzzling over for some time, an explanation as to why they sing at night, for hours on end, during the spring and summer. They were not singing for pleasure—that was a human presumption. They were singing out of desperation.

I discovered this unromantic fact more or less by accident the previous summer, when a pair of mockingbirds took possession of the tree next to my study. They also laid claim to my neighbor's backyard—and a choice bit of property it is. Neighbor Kay waters every few days, and the grounds are lush and green and tranquil. She pampers the marigolds and pansies in their beds along the edges of the lawn. She mows the lawn each Monday afternoon, always spiraling inward toward the center of the yard in carefully negotiated passes until, with a final charge, the machine devours the last shock of unkempt grass. This achieves the impeccable perfection of a putting green.

In the corner of the yard lies the garden plot. Kay has so thoroughly fertilized and stirred the soil that tomatoes cluster like grapes on the plants, the zucchini lie like seals on the ground, and lettuce, radishes, kohlrabies, and various spices and herbs stand in bushy rows. All is hidden from the world by a wall of shrubs and trees (penetrated only by the gap opposite my window). It is Kay's sanctuary. She doesn't realize it is also a paradise for the mockingbirds. But it is. It is ideal. It produces a whopping harvest of spiders and bugs. (The insects are a never-ending source of grief for Kay, and she turns piously to the gods of pesticide for protection; but the yard is too nutritious, and the ritual spraying of malathion seems to have had little effect on the multiplication of small creatures.)

Anyway, one night in July I was working late, and at around 2:00 A.M. it occurred to me that Jack, as I called the male, was becoming obnoxious. He had been singing without pause for at least an hour, his volume rising as the night wore on. Maybe his voice just *seemed* louder because the background noise was lower, but the fact was, my ears were actually fluttering with the sharp, choppy phrases that mockingbirds sing. The music of this legendary bird stands out chiefly for its volume and its coarse, relentless mimicry. A well-charged mockingbird throws into its song anything that comes to mind, including phrases from the local scrub jays, California quail, crows, cats, as well as phrases which are unrecognizable and may be original. Crows merge into quail, which become jays, which transform into cats, without any regard for harmony, transitional grace, development of theme, or musical plot. It is the avian equivalent of heavy metal.

But why was Jack singing at night in the first place? The sense of it was hard to see. For one thing, he was giving away his position to every cat for blocks around. For another, he was using energy. All that volume was generated by the laborious convulsions of Jack's diaphragm and breast muscles, and the cost in terms of metabolic economy had to be enormous. Birds of Jack's size sometimes eat twice their body weight in food each day, just to exist. It is the price of warm blood. In addition to gathering their own food, Jack and his mate (whom I could not resist naming Jill) were rearing chicks. Jack and Jill were locked into the frantic pursuit of energy, and yet here was Jack blaring forth throughout the night and most of the day. No bird would spend that kind of energy unless it was critically important.

I wondered if the racket might drive cats away. It was plausible. I am not exaggerating—the noise was up near the nuisance level. But no, it couldn't be a defense, otherwise every bird on the planet would have stumbled in the course of the eons upon the gambit of singing at night, loudly. Natural selection thrives on such discoveries. The din would be stupefying. No, the only reason I could see had to be competition with other mockingbirds. That would be easy to test. It would also be sweet fun: a tape recorder!

I set it in the window and began recording. A half hour later the tape ran out, and shortly after, Jack stopped for a breather, maybe even a nap.

Not, however, if I could help it. I turned the volume up and broadcast the same din he had just inflicted on me.

"CHIREEP, CHIREEP," went the tape.

There was a moment of silence. Then from the dark, thick blackness of the tree came: "*CHIREEP! CHIREEP!*"

Each phrase was an exact replica of his own recording. The only difference was the volume. Then it struck me that Jack was trying to outdo what he took to be a formidable rival.

"RASH, RASH, RASH," went the tape.

"*RASH! RASH! RASH!*" screamed Jack.

"TEREEK, TEREEK, TEREEK."

"*TEREEK!! TEREEK!! TEREEK!!*" gurgled Jack, almost strangling with the effort.

From my point of view it seemed a great joke, but to Jack it was not funny at all. It was probably the most desperate moment of his life—2:00 in the morning, a monstrous male in the immediate blackness challenging his reign, threatening to take his land, to dispossess his family, and there was no escape, nowhere to move and start over. Here was where he had to fight, to lodge the butt of his spear in the earth and make his stand. Well, by the gods of the bushes and the bugs, he was not going to go quietly.

"TERIPPA, TERIPPA, TERIPPA."

"*TERIPPA, TERIP*—" It could have gone on to the end of the tape, but I had my answer. Then, too, despite my grousing, I was actually fond of Jack. I turned the recorder off.

Simple as it was, the evidence revealed the true reality of a mockingbird's life. Like most songbirds, this species has evolved over the eons a system of parceling the land into territories. In a sense, a territory is a natural, self-actuated farm from which a pair gleans its living. Males compete to win a territory, then defend it, and the game never ends. The males rarely fight physically, because injury is too costly at a time when a bird needs all its energy, all its strength, just to break even in the economics of life. But if physical combat is too risky, singing is not, and the vigor and skill of a warrior's song give a good idea of his physical condition should it ever come to a showdown.

The plain truth was, in addition to making a living by hunting bugs and grubs, Jack was locked in musical combat for his family's survival. Singing was the measure of his substance and his grit, and his nightly performance proved to all his nearby rivals that he was bird enough to defend his property.

Conversely, if he got sick or was injured or just plain grew old, that would also come out in his song, and—I'm willing to bet—his neighbors would start to encroach. That could prove disastrous. Losing part of his farm could mean the difference between rearing two chicks, say, or three or four.

That's how things stood in my mind until that morning in October. I had just assumed that since mockingbirds sing to defend their territories during the breeding season, they would cease and desist during the off season. But here it was October, the chicks had long ago flown the nest, and yet the males were still holding forth. Not quite so emphatically, mind you, and they were not singing at night, but they were still territorial. Apparently the mockingbird has evolved a system of year-round residence—unusual for songbirds, but facts are facts.

Now, at the beginning of January, things are starting to heat up again. The young males— the ones coming up in the world—want to carve out their own territories, and the old incumbents like Jack are trying to hold them off.

The evidence is everywhere. This morning I got up and walked several blocks to buy a newspaper. The air washed damp and cool over my face, and the birdsongs twittered in my ears like a sprightly gigue. I looked up, and there was Jack perched on his telephone pole. His little gray body heaved and jerked as he belted out his song. I proceeded about a hundred yards and saw another mockingbird perched atop a telephone pole, carrying on with his own melody, just like Jack. I kept walking and pretty soon came to yet another mockingbird, likewise engaged, at which point a revelation struck, sweeping me high above the houses and their rectangular plots of land.

What I saw was no longer the artificial symmetry of my human neighborhood. It was an aerial view of Jack's world, a mosaic of organic principalities laid out among the bushes and trees and gardens and lawns, each created and defended through interminable bouts of sonic sparring, each producing the food and providing the shelter to sustain its feudal lord and his mate in perpetuity.

Suspended there over this alternate world, I rubbed my eyes in wonder. The immortal line from *Walden*, Henry David Thoreau's sermon on the pure and natural life, arose from memory. "The mass of men lead lives of quiet desperation," wrote Henry David, and I played it again, forward, then backward, for it struck me that Thoreau had misunderstood the creatures to whom he had listened for divination. It impressed him that ". . . after the evening train had gone by, the whippoorwills chanted their vespers for half an hour . . ."; it seemed to him that the squirrel, perched in the top of a pine, was ". . . chiding all imaginary spectators, soliloquizing and talking to all the universe at the same time. . . ."

To assume that wild creatures have the innate goodness, the in-nocent, uncontaminated inclination—to presume that they have even the time—to revel in vespers, soliloquies, and songs is the fan-tasy of the touring romantic. It is the nature of humans, weary of ceaseless conflict and yearning for escape, to see quaint custom in another culture's combat, to see the exercise of honor in the snarled challenge, to hear the dance in the wild shuffle of the duel. The truth is too harsh, too bright for the romantic mirror to reflect. The glass cracks on the impact of truth.

As the revelation passed, I shook my head and found myself once again on the sidewalk. I liked Thoreau, applauded his stand against materialistic stress, but couldn't help wondering how *Walden* would have turned out if he'd owned a tape recorder, even a little cheap one.

THE TENDER
MACHO
MEDFLY
MALE

On the island of Maui, on a certain fruit farm, in the foliage of a lemon tree, there lies an enchanted spot. The sun sprinkles down onto the leaves in a particular way, and every morning around nine o'clock male medflies start to arrive. Within five minutes they have all gathered, four to eight vigorous young bucks drawn together for one primal reason: the passing of the genes. Being medflies, they form a lek, a group of males who congregate on some communal grounds to attract females, compete for their favors, and carry out courtship.

No one knows why this particular eight-to-ten-inch sphere of space among the lemon leaves is so special to the gathered flies, but the quality of light seems to be a critical factor. There is something romantic about it, rather like the low lights associated with champagne. There is also a practical and mundane need for light, which

we will consider by and by. But beyond the matter of lighting it is difficult to divine the attractions of the lek location. The space holds
an inscrutable appeal.

A lek can be convened in various kinds of bushes or trees—in a
coffee bush, a mango tree, a peach tree—but there is usually a certain similarity to the settings. The lay of the land, the color and out-
line of the foliage, the kind of tree—these aspects probably all play
some role. But whatever the attraction is, the years pass, the flies
die, the leaves fall and new ones grow, and the next generation of
males gather on the next crop of leaves on the same hallowed spot in
the same wonderful tree every morning at nine. Then the prelimi-
naries begin.

At the center of the lek always hangs a single leaf that is, to a
medfly male, *the* place to be seen. This fits the ecological definition
of a competitive situation—a resource in short supply—because
the rules of medfly lekking call for just one male per leaf. Like males
everywhere, the medflies fight for what they covet. They butt heads
like minuscule rams until one is dislodged from the leaf; or, in what
looks like a contest of pure will, two approach, touch antennae, and
then sit there for about five minutes until one simply gets up and
leaves. How is this second kind of victory won? It is another mystery
of the lek.

When the fighting subsides, a territorial hierarchy has evolved:
the exalted central property is occupied by the king of the lek, with
the leaves of the lesser males arranged like planets around the sun.
The lek is now ready to perform. Each male takes his position, always on the underside of his leaf, and emits a scent—a "pheromone"—which commingles with the scent of the others and drifts
downwind. The eight male colognes all mixed into one cloud create
the olfactory chords necessary to arouse the female's passion. One
male, singing with a solo scent in the forest, would probably have
little chance of attracting a mate, for a single dose would not excite
her interest. Only the strong aroma of the group arouses her, be-

cause lekking is much more than a sexual convention: It is also a system for ensuring that the males are competitive, that there are winners present. This consideration is very important to a female medfly.

If she is ripe for courting, the female traces the aerial flow of pheromones back to the lek and heads straight for the prime, central real estate, where the dominant male awaits her visit. She has no interest in the surrounding properties: the other males are losers as far as she's concerned.

Now the second act begins, the ritual of courtship, and this is where the importance of lighting comes into play. The male, being on the leaf's underside, has no way of knowing a female has arrived unless the sunlight is falling on his territory. If so, the leaf glows like a monitor screen, and the female becomes a silhouette. This is the cue he's been waiting for. Immediately he aligns himself with her image so that the two are facing in the same direction. Then he pulls his abdomen under his body and begins to vibrate his wings. This action draws air from behind, adds a courtship pheromone as it passes by, and fans the perfumed breeze between his legs. The breeze wafts upward, curling around the edges of the leaf, and lures the female, who follows the scent back over the leaf's edge to the underside. She walks up to the male and stops about two millimeters away. There she stands, facing him head on, awaiting the next step in the courtship.

Still vibrating his wings, he begins to fan them back and forth in slow, beseeching strokes, a tremolo now superimposed on his gestures. At the same time he swivels his head from left to right and right to left in a rocking motion. To anyone who has never seen this performance, the wonder is difficult to describe, for thousands of tiny lenses comprise the medfly's eye. They serve as prisms which shred the spectrum into its various hues and beam them back to the world in a kaleidoscope of desire. Shimmering streaks of red transform to purple, purple turns to green, green to orange, orange to pink, pink to red, and so on across the rainbow with each turn of the male's head.

After several minutes of this scintillating appeal, however, the female may simply fly off and reject the male. About 10 percent of these dominant, virile males seem to have something wrong with their "moves." They may be invincible in male-to-male combat, but when it comes to charming the ladies, they prove to be objects of little appeal.

But there is still more to this courtship of the fruit flies. In the medfly, a strategy of choice seems to have evolved so that a female can reject a male at a number of points along the courting way, right up to the ultimate union. Apparently, this is why mating takes place on the underside of the leaf, for if, after receiving the sign of acceptance, the male mounts his intended too brusquely or makes a move that is in any way offensive, she simply lets go of the leaf and the couple tumble to the ground. Usually, this terminates the union.

Now, if we put the hand lens down and look at courting medflies from the long view, we see certain parallels to the human comedy. The most striking of these is the notion of the ideal American male—a creature which is simultaneously tough and tender.

He is the product of much intellectual groping and he has emerged slowly—"evolved" gives a better sense of the process, for evolution is change that is forced by changes in the world about. In this particular case, the evolution has occurred in splenetic fits and starts, the Valkyries of the women's movement zipping their arrows of discontent after the darting and weaving male; and, make no mistake, the attitude of women is a part of the world with which the human male has had to cope.

In the sixties and seventies the sociosexual theorists gnashed teeth and pondered and came up with a new ideal of masculinity. This was the tender, sensitive male. The creature quickly developed some major flaws, however, the most irritating of which was wimpiness. He wouldn't, or couldn't, play the male's traditional role, and qualities like stability, tolerance, honor, protection, and financial support soon started to erode. The new male was also reluctant to form commitments—and why should he? Sex was now free of charge.

In earlier times the price of sexual gratification was marriage, and marriage to one woman for an entire life was a game of endurance. It made for stoic men. The strong, silent types were strong partly because they were silent; silence conserved strength. However, what resulted from strong, silent characters were men of bronze. You needed a truck to move them. That was why the feminist theoreticians created their new ideal, who existed through the seventies.

As the eighties got under way, people turned their attentions more and more to themselves in the Me Generation, and the tender, sensitive, but vitiated man evolved into an even more bizarre creature, Narcissistic Man. Like his predecessor, the narcissistic male also proved unfit for life in the real world, and now, at the start of the nineties, the sociosexual theorists have finally combined the various ideals in their newest creation, Tender Macho Man.

The irony is that tender macho males are exactly what female medflies have demanded for tens of millions of years. They have exerted what is known as a selection pressure, so that the traits of the tender macho have been incorporated in his genes. I suspect that such qualities have also been encoded in the genes of many human males, needing only to be encouraged by female choice in order to develop. I believe this because of how female choice operates in the course of evolution.

When medflies gather to mate, two main forces are at work. The first is male competition. In order to have a chance of mating, a male must prove himself through the rough-and-tumble of the lek. Anyone who gains the central leaf is a winner who carries fit, competitive genes, and the property he owns attests to that fact. But strength, toughness, and competitive drive are only parts of a larger group of traits. A winner in the male games must also carry the genes for normal social behavior. In fruit flies there is no question but that behavior comes directly from the genes—because insects haven't got the intellect to learn manners. What a medfly does is therefore what he is, and when he crawls over to meet a female, his little leaf becomes a stage on which he reveals no less than his central essence: his genetic constitution.

Here the second force comes into play, the force known as female choice. By rejecting the male who doesn't satisfy her whims, the female rejects his genes and, gradually, over the eons, constructs the ideal male. Well, let us say one who meets her basic needs.

And what are the implications for the human condition? That the same forces that have shaped the medfly male have shaped his human cousin as well. That across the endless plains of time, human males courting human females have been accepted and rejected on the grounds of toughness *and* tenderness, and that the chosen males have passed to some of their sons the overall genetic stuff of good and balanced men. (Genetics is a tricky business, though, and good fathers often beget not-so-good sons. Not to mention the fact that some females prefer pure macho, and others prefer wimps, and so today, as the saying goes, "For every pot there's a lid.")

So, after all the shouting about sexual roles is over and done, after all the sexual theories and introspections, all the philosophizing and moralizing have been laid to rest, we've arrived back at the point through intellectual groping that medflies reached through genetic selection many million years ago. We males have had no choice. The females would not have it any other way.

GORILLA

MUMS

No one knows precisely what happened that afternoon, but it must have gone something like this. Dianne had been tending her baby like any loving mother with a three-day-old infant. At times she cradled him in her massive hairy arms and gazed at his tiny wrinkled face. Other times she sat and held him close so his little black lips could knead the milk from her nipple, his miniature hands resting on her breast as he worked. When she moved about she took him tenderly in the crook of her arm and walked carefully, supporting herself on one arm and two legs. For three intense days she had nurtured the child, the time made sharper, perhaps, by the memory of her first infant, born still. Except for the fact that she was separated from her friends and peers, it had been a good three days.

Now, however, it was the afternoon of July the Fourth, and the mood had shifted. The humans had started arriving early to picnic in the hills behind the Los Angeles Zoo, and their gabblings, laughs, shrieks, and carnal yawps drifted over the zoo grounds, punctuated by the popping of firecrackers and guns. As the day wore on, the noise seeped into her mind and became malaise. The once-comforting park was now sinister.

Then it caught on fire. Sparked by a cookout fire or a stray fire-cracker, the grass ignited and the flames slithered quickly over the hillside. Smoke billowed into the sky and drifted into the compound where Dianne was kept, separate from the other gorillas.

The significance of smoke to a caged animal is difficult for humans to comprehend, for the simple reason that we *can* comprehend. An animal cannot. It knows only the immediate fear, then the terror of what it does not grasp. To an animal, which cannot think in abstract symbols, fire is a living, supernatural thing. An animal cannot know that fire is anchored by the laws of chemistry to its oxidizing source; it cannot disengage the primal fears that drive its mind. Nor can it become arrogant in its grasp of natural law and smug in its technological power. It can only know that fire burns, and the only defense is distance. Add to this innocence the deep anxieties of motherhood, confine this mother with her infant behind the walls of a compound, surround her with smoke, sirens, crackling twigs and branches. Then face her with the flames.

The isolation made the situation even more horrific. Dianne had been separated from her peers to protect her and her infant from the possibility of in-group aggression. Now there was nowhere to turn for comfort. She could hear the group; they were just beyond the wall. But she could not touch them, could not draw comfort from the huge silverback male, could not see his chest-thumping, fang-baring response to danger.

Trapped in her animal fears, the hidden programs of survival came on line. She must have paced quickly back and forth along the walls, scanning the top for some breach, some handhold, some way to climb out of her cage and save her infant. But search as she might, she could find nothing. The walls could not be scaled.

Then the thing came. It came up low from the east, just above the treetops, preceded by a deep, droning growl but blocked from view by the trees. One instant all was clear; the next, all was obscured. It loomed over the trees, over the buildings, over the entire world. A pterodactyl? A primal ghost from the deep subconscious? The shape emitted a snarling, gut-wrenching roar so violent that the leaves rattled. Then, before the mother could even think of dashing for cover, the creature was gone, disappeared beyond the trees. It flew onward toward the smoke-roaring flames to dump its load of borate and water, to thrill the spectators, whose day had been made.

There is no doubt that Dianne panicked. In her arms she held not only her infant, but in her infant her genes, the driving force behind the will to live.

The next morning the infant was dead. Dianne had killed her own child. That, at least, is how it appears. Apparently, in lunging for cover, the terrified mother had swung her infant in a huge, powerful arc, accidentally bashing its head against a rock.

In cases like this where random events converge on one instant, people tend to shrug their shoulders and say, "Life is tough." It's comforting to know, then, that the infant's death was not in vain; for he brought out behavior in his mother that eventually helped to revolutionize the methods by which zoos breed gorillas. Before his brief existence it was assumed by the people in charge of gorilla reproduction that maternal skills had to be learned at the knee, so to speak, of experienced females. But the behavior of Dianne, who had been raised by zookeepers, indicated that maternal behavior either had deep innate roots, or it was guided by some process that mimicked the appearance of innate behavior. To sort out the truth, we must look to the history of gorillas in captivity.

Zoo breeding is a recent endeavor. The first gorilla ever born in captivity was delivered in the Columbus, Ohio, Zoo in 1956. Before that, all gorillas were captured in the wild as infants, wrenched away from their parents, who were killed during the acquisition, and raised like human infants by doting zookeepers. They matured into creatures that looked like normal gorillas, with the thick, squat bodies, the immensely muscled arms, coarse, dark fur, the great crest of bone ascending to a summit atop the skull, and the massive brows ossified across the front of the skull.

The appearance of normalcy, however, was deceptive. Behind those entrenched eyes lurked a mind suspended between the genetic nature of the gorilla and the alien culture of the human being. This misshapen mind hung there, over the abyss separating man from beast, and when such gorillas were placed together they often fought savagely, sometimes to the death, because they could not relate to others of their own kind.

After World War II, gorillas became easier to acquire, and they were often raised in pairs. That produced creatures with better social skills, and they could be held in the same enclosures, but they did not breed. They related to each other as siblings, not as objects of sexual desire.

The fact was, across the country gorilla programs were run in complete ignorance of normal gorillas. We knew nothing of their behavior in the wild—nothing of their social behavior and social structure, nothing of their mating habits, nothing of their parental techniques—and so the breeding program groped along slowly by trial and error.

Then came the remarkable studies of wild gorillas by George Schaller and Dian Fossey, naturalists who actually lived among the great apes. Their revelations began to revolutionize the way zoos dealt with gorillas, because re-creating the conditions in which wild gorillas live poses the ultimate goal of any zoo. Wild gorillas lived in small, intimate groups with one or two adult males accompanied by three to four or more females. The zoos, therefore, began to group their gorillas, too. That was when the pregnancies started to occur.

That was also when the question of how to raise the children became something of a quandary. Because apes are so patently similar to us humans, or, to be honest about it, because we are so similar to the other apes, the keepers of zoos assumed that the skills of mothering had to be learned. However, because zoo gorillas were reared by humans in unnatural conditions, the females never saw and never participated in the group dynamics of gorilla motherhood. Therefore, by any rational accounting, the females should not be suited for taking care of their own infants. This set up a self-fulfilling prophecy. If the gorillas could not care for their own infants, the zookeepers would have to step in and raise yet another generation under artificial conditions. Motherhood would never be learned.

The only chance of breaking the cycle was to risk the infant and see if, with zookeepers poised to intervene, a zoo-raised gorilla could acquire the skills of motherhood on her own. The gorilla chosen was Dianne; to everyone's surprise, she showed the basics of normal mothering, and the skills were so well formed that they seemed to be inborn. The ageless debate of nature versus nurture had headed on a perpendicular path toward nature. However, the evidence turned out to be not so simple. With Ellie it soon twisted back toward nurture.

Like Dianne, Ellie had been taken from the wild at about one and had been raised in the zoo. Inspired by Dianne's performance, the zoo officials decided to let Ellie rear her own child. That never happened. The keepers found the remains of her first infant, decapitated and thoroughly dismembered. The only question was whether the mother had murdered her infant or whether it had been stillborn and torn apart out of grief. After much agonizing, the officials decided to let Ellie try again, this time under close scrutiny. They were present when the next infant was born, but before they could intervene, Ellie tore off most of the infant's face, leaving no doubt about her maternal suitability.

If Dianne had cast a vote for inborn mothering skills, Ellie cast ten against. Ellie was sound of body; she was as fertile as potting soil and could produce more infants, which made her invaluable. Infant gorillas were selling at the time for around $75,000. But how to retrieve them intact from their mothers? The answer, of course, was caesarean section. Ellie's third child was transferred straight from her womb to the zoo's nursery. There he was named Caesar.

As the doors closed behind him, the breeding program returned to human surrogation. Innate mothering skills did not exist in Ellie, and one had to doubt that they existed in the majority of other zoo-reared gorillas. Perhaps most mothers *did* have to be reared in the presence of maternal gorillas in order to learn the skills of mother-hood. At $75,000 per baby, the zoo's policy shifted back to hand-rearing its little gorillas.

Meanwhile, things had changed in the nursery program. Obser-vations in the wild revealed the crucial need for early social contact, so the protocol now called for rearing the infant gorillas together. Even if they could not experience the natural life of the group, at least they could experience each other. This led to the next gener-ation of gorilla mums, which included a young female named Cleo.

As a member of the first zoo-born generation, Cleo went to the nursery at birth and was raised for two years with a male named Bru-tus, one of her half-brothers. The two were inseparable, literally, and Thaya Dubois, Assistant Director of Research, remembers them as a single ball of black fur, asleep in each other's arms.

From the beginning Cleo was extremely good-natured; when she was introduced to the older gorillas, she adapted to the group almost without effort. She also remained on remarkably docile terms with her keepers.

Cleo was a precocious child and by the age of five she was men-struating, ovulating, and instigating what were called "play copu-lations" with two of the young males in her group. At the age of six she copulated with Chris, the huge and dominant male, but Chris was using real ammunition. When she became pregnant the zoo of-ficials decided that if ever there were to be a candidate for natural motherhood, Cleo was it. Her personality seemed stable, and she

was so cooperative that she would probably accept human instruc-
tion in the proper care and handling of her infant. Should she hold
the infant upside down the gorilla keepers could take it from her and
demonstrate the right position. If the infant was crying for food, the
keepers would show her how to nurse. Eight and one-half months
later, on the morning of April 11, 1987, the keepers arrived at the
zoo to find Cleo holding, nursing, and taking expert care of a fine little lad who was later named Kelly. It was clear to all that Cleo was
doing just fine on her own and needed no lessons in mothering.

Several months later Sandy, Cleo's own mother, gave birth to an
infant girl, to be named Angel. After a few days of holding little Angel upside down, or holding her too far down on her fat torso for the
infant to reach a teat—after a somewhat clumsy start, Sandy, too,
became a proficient mother. (Angel was Sandy's third child, but the
first she was allowed to rear; the keepers feel that she might have
learned from watching her daughter handle Kelly.) On August 1,
Evelyn, another zoo-reared female, gave birth to Jim. She, too,
seemed to have perfect mothering technique right from the start.
Cleo and Evie, both zoo-reared with other infant gorillas, appeared
to possess innate mothering skills.

Which brings us back to the question of nature versus nurture.

This is always a loaded question, but when nature and nurture
converge on the apes, the chauvinist human truly begins to squirm.
Subconsciously we all know how closely related, and therefore how
similar, we members of the apes are, and this places us in a philosophic dilemma.

If, for instance, we find that apes depend nearly as much on
learned behavior as do humans, it confirms our kinship, but it also
threatens our self-proclaimed status as rulers of the planet. If we and
the apes are *too* similar, how can we kill them in the wild and annex
their land? How can we cage them in zoos and how can we dissect
and inject and wire and poison and infect them to certain, calcu-

lated death in the quest for scientific knowledge? How can we deprive them of everything if they are so nearly equal to us?

On the other hand, if we set the apes too far from us, this also threatens the illusion of human superiority. Why would gorillas like Cleo, Evie, Sandy, and Dianne depend so heavily on learning for all their other behaviors, but rely on innate programs for maternal care? Is it possible that the innate structure of our own brains plays a much greater role in the processes of intellection than we want to believe?

The apes suggest such things. When a captive gorilla or a chimpanzee or an orangutan, with a host of humans peering across the moat, calmly begins to masturbate, or when a female chimp with enormously swollen genitals presents her merchandise to the dominant male, and he inspects the offering with microscopic interest and both hands, or when a big gorilla charges wildly around his compound, heaving feces at the crowd and hooting exuberantly, or when he delicately manipulates a twig into his mouth, savoring it like the most sophisticated chef, or when he gazes thoughtfully back at the people on the other side of the moat—when the ape acts out his mind with the most complete insouciance, he parodies his hairless cousins, taunts us, accuses us, and if you stop to think on it, reflects us. He communicates on the deepest levels, across the eons, across the illusory chasm that *Homo sapiens* fancies between himself and other species. Deep down inside we know that there, but for a few crucial genes, go we, and some of us, I know on good authority, curse their luck. Our vaunted superiority—what is that? Why, it is little more than a cap of self-consciousness and extreme cleverness woven into one cloth. The cap sits like a beanie atop the exact same emotions that guide our close kin. Therefore, in the illusion of human divinity, the lubricious pleasures of sex must be indulged behind closed doors. The animal urges must be euphemized; angers, aggressions, urges, lusts—call them motives, desires, and goals.

And above all, it must be proclaimed to the world that the human is the only animal whose actions are guided by reason. These are the kinds of unspoken concerns that inform our dealings with the anthropoid mind.

Two hypotheses have been put forth to explain the seemingly innate nature of Cleo's, Evie's, Sandy's, and Dianne's maternal skills.

Thaya Dubois, who has worked daily with the gorillas for nine years, simply says that what you see is what you see. The behavior is innate. It is generated from within without benefit of prior experience. This is the opinion of someone who has pondered the problem without allegiance to one explanation or another and is willing to conclude whatever the evidence indicates.

"No, that's not right," says Warren Thomas, director of the zoo and a veterinarian by training. "In humans and apes the maternal *urge* is innate, but the *behavior* is learned."

When asked how he explains the astonishing performance of the four mother gorillas, he says, "Let's look a little closer at this. Gorillas are like humans; there's a big range of intelligence. Some females are just brighter than others: they can figure out what to do so quickly that it *looks* like innate behavior. The dumber ones have to learn from watching others."

It's not an implausible argument, and Thomas may be right, as far as he goes. But his argument has retreated from the original doctrine of learning at momma's knee to what he alleges is learning on the spot. The argument has retreated so far that it finds itself rubbing shoulders with innateness again. The innately smart versus the innately dumb. Besides that, the idea of instantaneous learning seems to be a case of reaching for answers. "Intuitive insight" would be a more apt term.

There are other holes in Thomas's view. If the mothering urge is innate, what about Ellie, who tore apart her infants at birth? There is reason to suspect that her traumatic past twisted her instincts, so the urges that Thomas claims to be innate may be deeply affected by rearing, and the mothering skills he claims are learned may be profoundly affected by an acquired shape of the mind.

Thaya Dubois freely admits that the innate part of mothering skills is not so simple as the word "innate" implies. Upbringing plays a critical role; if it did not, then gorillas would have the proper urges and the proper skills, no matter how they were raised.

To put it all in perspective, let us review the evidence. The first generation of mother gorillas were taken from the wild and reared artificially, without contact with other gorillas for the first few years. At the Los Angeles Zoo, these mothers included Dianne, Sandy, and Ellie. Sandy and Dianne were able to care for their offspring, but both started off with relatively crude skills, later refined by practice. With Ellie, the question of learned motherhood never had a chance to be asked because in place of the urge to mother was the urge to murder. This is not to say that Ellie's background was totally to blame; she may have had psychotic tendencies, as do some humans; she may have been extraordinarily sensitive to childhood trauma; in short, her genetics may have been her fate. But in all three examples a case can be made for significant affect of nurture: the loss of parents, the brutal removal from the wild, and, especially, the rearing apart from other gorillas.

All of this squares with the classic studies on rhesus monkeys by psychologist Harry Harlow. Professor Harlow reared monkeys in various degrees of social deprivation, including some who were placed with surrogate mothers fashioned from chicken wire. These infants grew into psychologically twisted adults who could not function in monkey society. They sat alone, embracing themselves and rocking back and forth all day long. They were never able to breed.

Early gorilla care seems to have affected the first generation of zoo gorillas in a similar way. In zoos across the country, gorillas isolated from their peers as infants have ended up as socially incapacitated creatures who could not interact normally with others. A significant number became antisocial misfits inclined toward violence and foul moods and rendered incapable of courtship and breeding behavior, much less motherhood.

Cleo and Evie, on the other hand, showed virtually perfect mothering skills. The skills appeared spontaneously and gave every indication of being innate. And if they were learned from a quick assessment of the situation, then the ability to size things up may have been brought out by a better upbringing.

What emerges from all this is that there comes a point where nature and nurture become the same thing; you cannot separate them. Instantaneous learning, or intuition, versus innate generation—how can they be distinguished? The difference is semantic. Nor can nature and nurture be ranked as to which contributes the greater share to motherhood. Both contribute 100 percent. This is made absurdly obvious when you consider the meaning of the word "nurture." It strongly connotes food. The genes provide the blueprint and the machinery for metabolic growth; the food supplies the substance and the fuel. Without genes you would not have a gorilla; without food you would not have a gorilla.

On the subtler grounds of behavior the best explanations of nature and nurture take into account an idea that might be called evolutionary crafting. Almost all creatures have been crafted by natural selection to live in a particular environment. But this purpose has a flip side, which is this: not only has the creature been designed to live in a particular kind of environs, but it *has* to live there. It can survive only in the environment for which it has been designed.

This is a concept to which most humans are completely oblivious. The average American is said to spend 98 percent of the time indoors; the purpose of civilization is to insulate us from nature; therefore, Western civilization is essentially a moon base, and because we can build moon bases anywhere, it is difficult to imagine what it is like to be restricted to life in a particular kind of place by your form and the workings of your mind.

Most other creatures, however, are so intimately calibrated to their ancestral environs ("niche" is the ecological term) that, to put it bluntly, they are dead when taken from it. The beached whale and the drowned rat are classic examples. A rat or a cockroach crossing a street, for which neither was designed, is a little less obvious, but an example nonetheless of what happens upon leaving the genetically assigned niche.

As for the gorilla, a creature designed to live with a group of its own kind in a tropical rain forest, it is reasonable to assume that little gorillas should be raised in jungles, or at least in surroundings that resemble or suggest jungles. Above all, little gorillas must be raised with some semblance of normal social interaction. The genes "expect" to receive certain kinds of experience, that is, nurture; the genes are crafted to receive it. When normal nurture is received, it interacts with the genetic program and leads to the growth of a normal gorilla.

If, however, gorillas are reared in isolation from their peers, the alien environment pulls nature from its genetically ordained course. Perhaps that is why Sandy and Dianne, both reared in isolation from other gorillas, performed clumsily and needed time to learn the mothering skills—to build what was not built in the course of normal events. Cleo and Evie, who were reared under more normal conditions, performed perfectly. Whether it be innate skill, or intuition, or instantaneous learning—call it what you will—the fact remains that when reared in social contact with other gorillas, young mothers appear to be fundamentally improved. Is the basic function of the intellect, the mind, affected by abnormal nurture? It seems like a real possibility.

POSTSCRIPT

The setting is the gorilla grotto at the Los Angeles Zoo, and the date is mid-July, 1987. Cleo has given birth to her son, Kelly, two and one-half months before; Evie and Sandy are due to give birth in a matter of weeks. Thaya Dubois is happily telling us about the birth and how it is affecting the adult gorillas.

Presently, the group are resting. Aristotle (nicknamed Chris), the silverback male, is lying on his side, head nestled blissfully on a boulder, which serves as the ideal pillow. From time to time he wrinkles his massive, hairy brow and scratches at the flies crawling about his dreams. He awakens for a moment, stretching his arms as if to embrace the sky. His jaw drops open in a cavernous yawn, with fangs protruding like stalactites and stalagmites. He squints out through a soporific blear at the humans, who are feeling but denying their simian kinship, and he rolls over and goes back to sleep.

The females rest in a group off to the side of the grotto, in an airy cave with concrete arches at the entrance. The scene suggests a porch and veranda, a family of gorillas lounging away the afternoon by watching people walk up and down their street. A few are snoozing, a few reclining against the cool concrete and drawing the occasional branch through their mouths, from one side to the other, to strip off the leaves. They smack their lips, lazily examine the stripped twig, and toss it away. Kay, another member of the group, is propped up against the rear wall, her eyelids drooping as she nods off to sleep. Sandy lies on her back next to Kay, her arm crooked over her head, her legs up on a boulder-ottoman, contemplating. And of course, there is Cleo, sound asleep on her back with her tiny son slumbering on her great, bone-buttressed cage of a chest, his right hand on her breast.

Thaya Dubois is ecstatic over the mother's success. It opens a whole new realm, an artificial niche, for the gorilla to occupy should it die out in the wild, as it inevitably will in the face of unchecked, uncheckable human population growth.

"Cleo has done such a spectacular job! It's beyond all our expectations. She's done so well with the handling, you'd think she was experienced. She even leans in and gives it little kisses on the head."

The allegation of kisses seems a bit schmaltzig, and Ms. Dubois is quick to defend it. "At first we thought she was just getting lint off, but you can see it on the film. She puckers her lips. It's a real, bona fide kiss."

The addition of little Kelly has had a significant and interesting impact on group dynamics, changing the group's overall mood, strengthening its unity. Before the infant's birth, the gorillas were essentially an aggregation, with the various individuals scattered here and there in the course of passing through life. Now they sit close together. Even the massive male has been affected and stays much closer to the others, which has greatly relieved the zoo officials.

"Everyone was worried about how he'd take this," declares Thaya Dubois, "and he wasn't let out for a couple of weeks after the baby was born, to make sure everything was stable. On the first day it was beautiful. Cleo went right up to him, as if to show him the baby. He looked at it and sat down next to her. He's just been wonderful."

The only dissonance has come from an adolescent male named Caesar. He is another half-brother of Cleo's and one of her lifelong playmates. He has found the sudden appearance of Cleo's tiny companion difficult to countenance.

"He seemed jealous. He'd run by and throw branches at her and pop her on the head and do lots of little nasty things. Nothing terribly aggressive, but just enough to be annoying and to say 'I don't like this baby.'"

The problem has been resolved by moving Caesar to another group in the adjacent enclosure. This decision was expedited by Caesar himself, after he climbed out of Cleo's enclosure in what appears to have been a jealous snit.

And so the gorilla breeding program seems to be moving in positive directions. Eleven-year-old Evie will probably be the next to give birth and is enduring the traditional trials of pregnancy.

"She used to be the wisenheimer of this group," explains Ms. Dubois. "She was always active and moving about, but now she keeps to herself. I'm sure she has morning sickness."

A glance at Evie confirms this prognosis. If ever there was a disheveled and patently miserable gorilla, it is this prospective mother sitting against a rock, legs akimbo before her, arms clasped around her midriff, staring off into the distance.

"Poor Evie," commiserates Thaya Dubois, herself a mother of two. "She used to be a wild kid."

IN
THE REALM
OF THE
ROOF RAT

It was a clear and balmy night. The wedding guests stood in groups sipping California Coolers and making polite conversation. The moon, a great silver disk with the Mare Serenitatis etched in its surface, was rising over the back alley, and a thick power line was dividing it into halves. People basked in the intimate, backyard ambience. The spell was then disrupted by a loud gasp, followed by a horrified exclamation.

"Oh, *gross!*"

"Revolting!" came a second opinion, followed by a "How tacky" from someone else.

Looking up, I saw a creature the size of an Idaho potato running along the power line above us. It traversed the cable with the virtuoso, almost mechanical certainty of a remote-controlled toy, and then (maybe it was the comments—the sounds, probably, not the words), just as the creature reached the midpoint of the yard, it stopped, absolutely motionless, in the center of the moon. It sat there, a black silhouette in a round frame, swaying gently on the Edison line. There was only one creature it was likely to be, and that was the roof rat, *Rattus rattus*, known in Europe as the black rat, purveyor of the plague.

Several seconds of astounded silence. The bride's father, a tall, balding, fanatically fit, marathon-running airline corporate executive—a man accustomed to giving orders and controlling things and assuring the best for his little girl—this man was now pacing with his face toward the moon, growling something about all the possible nights in the year and a gun. Then, without any forewarning even to my own mind, I heard myself blurt out, "What a wonderful thing!"

Another stunned silence, followed after several seconds by "pervert" muttered somewhere near the wedding cake. A rat could be excused, but a statement like this, in polite society, at the start of a marriage, was entirely inappropriate.

Yet the remark had just escaped. Thirteen years as a biologist had expanded my values, and what I saw suspended above the party was a masterpiece of evolution, a living thing which had been genetically calibrated to thrive in the nest of its most formidable enemy, the self-anointed pinnacle of evolution, *Homo sapiens*. The rat was doing splendidly, as illustrated by this individual above us, brazenly insulting our civilized sensibilities.

Even its scientific name, *Rattus rattus*, belies success. Identical names for genus (first name) and species (second) means that the species *rattus* was the first member described in the genus. In fact, Carl von Linne, the great systematist also known as Linnaeus, included *R. rattus* as a charter member of his classic work *Systema Naturae*. *Systems of Nature* set out to catalogue all creatures, but it started with the ones nearest at hand and most common.

I deeply appreciate another aspect of the roof rat's success, and it has to do with the notion of the niche. In straight English, the niche is where the animal lives and how it manages. Unlike us humans, who put clothes on and take them off, who live our lives inside artificial constructions, who carve and mold the earth to suit our desires, animals are designed for coping directly with a narrow slice of reality. Their bodies are therefore highly specialized.

Look at any part of the body—the leg, for instance. A leg like the kangaroo's is made long and springy, strung taut with tendons and wrapped tight with ligaments for serial bounding; the leg of the mole is made thick, short, and armed with stout, blunt claws for gouging through the soil; the seal's leg has been flattened and streamlined into a flipper for swimming. The principle holds without exception throughout an inventory of many millions of species.

Here, then, was this rat, this shape, levitated in the moon, displaying the form, the size, the habits—the overall life strategy—to survive in the attics, sheds, garages, and, especially, the shrubbery we have provided it. No poison, no gun, no extermination program has ever been able to eliminate its kind.

I understood the rat in great part because of a conversation I had had with a biologist named Tony Recht. Recht is actually what you'd call a modern naturalist; he's interested in the complete animal living in its natural world, and he uses modern technology to study it in its daily life. Several years ago he decided to outfit roof rats with little radio transmitters and follow them around, twenty-four hours a day, to see how they made their living. Where did they go and when, what did they eat and do? The radio technology itself was not a major problem, because Recht is an expert tinkerer. He is also dead serious about his work, and it was with a straight, almost grim, face that he persuaded an entire block of homeowners (only one refused) to let him appear at any hour of the day or night in their backyards. Thus it was that Recht could appear at three or four in the morning, clambering over fences, running along walls, sneaking under telephone lines, all the while carrying a Panasonic radio and pointing the antenna in the general direction of a rat.

The fact is, a neighborhood is an ecosystem. Natural laws operate there. It is a place where animals, if they can take advantage of the niche, can survive and multiply. Consider, for example, the realm of the bougainvillea. this vinelike shrub grows up walls, drapes over trellises and fences, and, in time, becomes a dense, tangled, thorn-studded mass several meters across. If a creature is curious enough to enter the structure, it will find that the outside layer of leaves and twigs is a soft shell six to eight inches thick, and it shields the interior from sun, wind, and rain. Inside is a grand auditorium, the space braced with branches, the roof interwoven with twigs and leaves; it is a utopia where cats, dogs, owls, and hawks never intrude, the sun never shines, the rain barely drips. In a land like this, a rodent can travel with easy confidence and rear a family in peace and tranquility. Human structures like run-down sheds, unused attics, and loosely stacked woodpiles strike the roof rat as even finer habitations. Consider an entire human neighborhood, and what you have is a virtual rat metropolis, linked together by the freeways of the telephone cables, the backyard fences, and the internuncial branches of trees.

As Recht discovered, in designing the roof rat for life in the camp of the humans, evolution has hit upon several key attributes. Size is one. An uninvited guest with the appeal of a rat must be able to hide in cracks and crannies. Color—or, actually, the lack of it—is also important. It's no accident that the rats are a neutral gray: they literally disappear in the shadows.

Then there's the matter of diet. A successful rat must first be attracted to the same items its host eats, then be able to digest them. Roof rats dearly love human treats like peanut butter. Here in Southern California they feed mostly on walnuts, avocados, pomegranates, apricots—typical backyard produce. Ivy shoots, with a few snails thrown in for protein, may round the diet out.

(These preferences appear to be genetically programmed. Recht found that the wood rat, *Neotoma fuscipes*, a native American species which shies away from human habitations, finds hibiscus flowers totally unappealing. The roof rat, on the other hand, dearly loves these blossoms and devours them like candy. It is no coincidence that humans have cultured hibiscus for centuries.)

But behavior is probably the most important factor in designing a rat for life in human society. To make a career of living among the enemy, the roof rat must have the right habits, the right reactions, and the right kind of intelligence. Learning requires experience, and in a world crawling with cats the truly vital skills—stealth, alertness, shyness—can be taught only with fatal risk. A rat gets no second chance. Its temperament and habits have therefore been genetically wired to fit the roof rat's niche as superbly as the body does.

For example, roof rats are compulsively arboreal; they shun the ground at almost all costs and live in the dense shrubbery, the trees, the attics, the jumbled woodpiles. (By contrast, the Norway rat, *Rattus norwegicus*, sometimes called by its less romantic name of sewer rat, stays almost exclusively on the ground. In that way the two species, which often live in the same neighborhood, have divided up a prime environment so as to minimize competition.) Roof rats use power lines, telephone wires, and fence tops for high-speed travel, scurrying quickly across the open spaces between feeding grounds. They follow daily patterns and make nightly rounds, taking the same pathways between points of interest.

They are also extremely wary. If you were to try trapping one and failed, it would not reenter the same trap. And if you were to disturb their nest area—if you rummaged through the attic, for instance—they would clear out; left undisturbed for about a week, they would return. Indeed, if you see one at all, it's probably because of overpopulation. Crowded conditions force the rats to forage longer and take more risks.

Knowledge of these traits can aid in rat control. Block off the elevated pathways; cut back trees so they don't bridge buildings; get rid of woodpiles, screen off holes into the house, cut down the ivy and bougainvillea. Do all this and you will drive roof rats from the area. You will drive them from the area because you have changed the niche. And that brings me back to the fact that creatures are crafted, body and soul, to *fit* their niches. Flip the coin over, and you will find a different law inscribed: as a creature is built for a particular purpose, so its life is held within the limits of its construction.

I ruminated on that law awhile, under the rat, and inevitably my mind drifted back to my own species. If this rat was crafted in body and soul to fit its niche, so too was *Homo sapiens* crafted to build and inhabit *its* niche. What did that say about its brain, about its mind?

Ah, the brain of *Homo sapiens*. It, too, was designed to cope with its niche, with its environment. And by far the most dominant, most threatening thing in that niche is other *H. sapiens*, a reality our brain must have been wired to reflect. The evidence is easy to see. When insulted or challenged, the brain gets angry. When flattered or rewarded or otherwise stroked, it gets happy. It gets suspicious when it detects the slightest hint of a hostile strategy; gets sexually aroused when . . . whenever. It becomes humble when overwhelmed by earthly circumstance; pious when faced with eternity; analytic when a problem looms; warlike when its nation sees the need. As for learning and experience, that, it seems, is superimposed on the deep wiring of the brain. Learning refines and calibrates the basic reactions, urges, impulses—the basic directions needed to survive among humans. It all traces back to the fact that the human brain was built for a niche. And that is why I stood there transfixed and why my admiration blurted out.

So there I stood, isolated in thoughts and social disgrace while the rat sat framed by the moon, its tail hanging down like a cord plugged into the darkness. Finally, after a minute or so, the host could stand it no longer. Grabbing a California Cooler, he poured it into a plastic cup.

"Stand back!" said he, and heaved the liquid up toward the rodent.

Alcohol is one substance that no civilized wild rat will tolerate, and this fellow seemed to anticipate the wobbling, rising globules. In a farewell display of fitness it sprinted out of the moon and scurried down the cable toward a loquat tree in the corner of the yard. A few rustlings, and it was gone. A rat had come, seen, been seen, been routed. That was all the people knew.

The reception never regained its spirit. Despite a dogged determination to send the newlyweds off in the California style, a somber mood pervaded the conversation; we all knew, instinctively if not consciously, that this niche we took for granted was not ours exclusively. The roof rat was at least as suited to it as we. I looked up at the cable supplying the house with electric nurture, and one last thought occurred: The rat, in adapting to this niche, in many respects mimicked its human host. It ate the same diet, inhabited the same buildings, used the same grounds. It had, in fact, become so similar that it is now used universally in science as an experimental surrogate. That is why the experimental results assume medical value. The ghost of William Carlos Williams, poet and physician, whispered the ultimate line from "Pastoral":

"These things astonish me beyond words."

DRACULA
STUMBLES
INTO BED

They came floating toward us at dusk, flapping side by side in long, ragged rows five hundred feet up, big black creatures with a wingspan of at least three feet. For a fractured second they were geese, but that was absurd: They were issuing from a grove of eucalyptus and palms. The grove towered above an endless arid plain of a different eucalypt species, skimpy, sparse, skinny, rooted in a hard, sandy soil littered with dry, brittle eucalypt leaves and nothing else, an expanse stretching southward to the treeless ocean of sand and rock of the Australian outback. The temperature stood at 103°F. It was not a place for geese.

The creatures had no visible neck, just a large round head. They had no visible tails and flew with a shambling motion, slow, deliberate, with a sloppy disregard for disciplined formations. They flopped across the sky like big moths, or owls (for a moment I considered that —but there are no social owls; owls are intensely independent and would never join a flight group). They drew closer.

Then that metamorphic instant came when the conscious mind knows.

Bats.

Of course—flying foxes, fruit bats. As so often in my education, I had read about them, had studied scientific papers on their social organization and their heat-regulating physiology, but I had never seen one. In my mind was an intellectualized bat, a scientific automaton constructed of mechanistic facts that did not add up to the sum of its living parts. Not to say that that was bad or uninteresting; it was not. After a quick information search, for instance, I recalled that these were members of the Megachiroptera, a group of 165 species that rely solely on sight for aerial navigation. The other 680-odd species of bats are called the Microchiroptera, because most of them are small to tiny. These bats hunt insects for the most part, although some hunt frogs or other items like fish, and they perceive the world by beaming ultrasonic pulses into the void and reading the echoes. Not so the megachiropterans: most use their eyes, and they eat fruit, leaves, nectar, pollen. They are vegetarians.

On they came, thousands upon thousands streaming from the eucalyptus-and-palm grove and stringing out loosely across the sky. Formation upon formation rowed through the air, passing over our heads toward some location where they would probably browse on the blossoms of the bloodwood tree, on the tender tips of new vegetation, or on wild fruits; sweeping away into the sunset, to begin what for them was a new day. At that point the reality of the southern hemisphere finally seeped into my conscious mind, the true magnitude of the little, subtle, yet immense and blatant differences that lie hidden everywhere and reveal the truth of where one stands on the planet.

I was traveling with photographer Peter Menzel, on assignment for *Smithsonian* magazine, and for the past four days we had been driving north in our Toyota Land Rover on the Stuart Highway. We had covered all but several hundred of the fifteen hundred miles between Adelaide and Darwin and were looking forward to the end of our journey.

The southern hemisphere had begun teasing me as soon as I landed in Sydney and disembarked among people who looked and dressed much like Americans but spoke with an irreproducible nasal twang. Sydney was a generic example of Western civilization, rumbling with traffic, jackhammers, high-rise construction, and pedestrians, but for some reason it confused me. I would walk to some downtown shop and be unable to find my way back without asking directions. I sat in a café one day and could have sworn by the feeling and direction of the sunlight that it was 10:30 in the morning, but in fact it was 3:30 in the afternoon. Then I realized it was the sun. It traveled across the northern sky, not the southern as in the United States, and I relied on that simple fact in a subconscious way. I had always had a good sense of direction, but now I had to think of the map, had to reason out my position, to correct for this solar disorientation.

After meeting with Menzel, I had flown to Adelaide, rented the Toyota, and driven off into the outback. We discovered that the strangeness pervaded the natural world too. For days we drove through desert that looked and seemed like the deserts of the American southwest in which I had grown up. The same arid, naked earth stretched for miles—except this earth was relentlessly red. Shadows cast by trees, rocks, ant mounds, buildings all extended south, not north as they would at home. The same gray, wispy foliage grew on the desert plants—but when you stopped for a closer look, the species were entirely unfamiliar. The mesquite turned out not to be mesquite at all, but some species of mulga; the creosote bushes were not creosote but various species whose names I was never able to learn.

And so it was when I met the animals. The lizards of the outback looked remarkably similar to their northern cousins of the Mojave and Colorado deserts. To the untrained eye their markings, their color schemes, size, and shape were virtually interchangeable. But they represented different families and could not have had any genetic connection for the last forty or fifty million years, not since Australia had broken free of the Antarctic and the South American land masses. The different lines of saurian descent had therefore converged on these colors and designs, nudged to a common end by the similar forces of similar lands. The process is called convergent evolution.

As an example, creatures as remotely related as bats, birds, and pterodactyls have entered the air by discovering independently, at vastly different times, the same physical forms and devices. Devices that work. Everywhere I looked in the Australian desert I saw the evidence of this process, a sublime example being the thorny devil. The average resident of the American southwest would call it a horned lizard or horny toad, which it is not. It is a thorny devil. It has just evolved the same spiky, armored look, the same blotchy markings and coloration, the same size. They live in the same kind of sandy places and eat the same diet, ants.

On the other hand, aside from the cattle and horses, which were extremely common (cattle in particular), the big creatures of the outback were strikingly different from those of the American deserts. Take the kangaroos, for example. On rare occasions we saw them standing out in the bush, propped on their tails, watching the Toyota go by. A few times we saw them springing along in that great, bounding lope of theirs (which has been evolved independently by our North American kangaroo rats and mice). But mainly we saw them lying dead in the road. The occasional emu, the Australian ostrich, also ended up adhering to the road, as did a few camels and water buffalo.

The birds were exotic and wonderful—one could honestly say fabulous. The most striking were the parrots: sulfur-crested cockatoos, black cockatoos (in the north), large flocks of gray-and-pink

cockatoos known as gallahs, parakeets, cockatiels, rainbow lori-
keets. Off in the bush were birds that looked like flycatchers but
weren't, birds that looked like warblers but weren't, along with crows
and ravens and eagles that were crows and ravens and eagles but of
different species than at home—everywhere I looked were birds
that resembled my old friends from North America, but weren't.

Pressing relentlessly north through the reversed desert, beneath
the reversed sun, with its reversed shadows, on the left side of the
highway, with the driver on the right fumbling and grinding the left-
hand gearshift, we passed through Alice Springs, twenty-five thousand Western Caucasians clustered with possibly a few thousand
Aborigines exactly in Australia's center—if the town were a titanic
axle, the continent would rotate smoothly around it—and then we
encountered the first of the termite mounds.

Like miniature smokestacks, up to three feet high and built of red
clay, they reminded me of industrial structures—which, of course,
they were. The first ones were bluntly rounded at the peak and devoid of architectural frills. But the farther north we drove the more
ambitious the forms became, each species constructing its own
mounds peculiar in shape, size, and texture. Some were thin and
sharply pointed, four to five feet tall, with a bubbled texture like
dripped wax and the overall look of Giacometti sculptures. Others
appeared to be constructed of large lumps, like enormous scoops of
ice cream, stacked as high as ten feet and weighing hundreds, perhaps thousands, of pounds. As we drove ever north these monuments to the pinnacle of cockroach evolution—for that is what termites are, the descendants of the roach—stretched off into the
distance like thousands upon thousands of military gravestones. For
hundreds of miles we passed among them, the representation of labor so persistent, so relentless, performed by laborers so multitudi-
nous that they affected the earth itself. The termites play the same
role in Australia that the wildebeest and other herbivorous herds

play in Africa: the role of primary consumers, creatures charged with clearing the ever-growing vegetation and delivering it back to the earth as chemical nutrient.

On they went, without beginning, without end, until our perceptual faculties began to quiver in the flow and stupendous objects began to appear. Elephants stood upright on a single leg, Aunt Jemimas stared through the branches of mulga brush, soldiers stood at attention, Smokey the Bear lurked next to the trunk of a eucalypt tree, and the ultimate sight, the Madonna, baby on lap. (I saw that. Menzel couldn't. The eye of the camera is too objective.)

I have wondered from time to time why the Madonna transmogrified that particular mound, why it appeared in that particular place, for it presaged the supreme glory of the Australian termite, the cathedral mound. If the other mounds had astounded us in their sheer multitudes, the cathedral mounds overwhelmed us with their monumental mass and their inspired architecture. Towering above us, ten, fifteen, even twenty feet into the sky, spires descended into flying buttresses, flying buttresses supported transepts, transepts crossed naves, naves ran parallel to cloisters.

Gazing up at these Gothic civilizations, up at tens of tons of earth mixed with hundreds of gallons of salivary mortar, built according to the genetic blueprint suffusing the unself-conscious minds of countless generations of crawling workers, you could not help—the thought was simply ineluctable—comparing the accomplishments of the two species, *Homo sapiens* and *Nasutitermes triodiae*. Time and again our minds returned to this exercise, and with the miles creeping past and Menzel driving, I found myself with notepad in hand, calculating the facts. The mounds were built by creatures no more than a quarter-inch long, with nothing but the efforts of their bodies. The Empire State Building, which represents an adequate entry in the competition, was built by human males averaging about five feet, nine inches long, aided and enormously abetted by hundreds of tools and the energy of fossil fuel channeled through modern machinery. Scaling the efforts of the two species according to body size, I concluded that a twenty-foot cathedral mound stood 960 termite-lengths in height, while the Empire State Building equaled the height of a mere 174 human males. The comparison does not do the termite justice.

We came at the end of that day to a sign that read "Mataranka Hot Springs, 7 km." The wind blowing from the south was as hot and dry as the wind from a smelter. A hot springs was not the ideal destination. But we had reservations in the hotel there and turned off to follow the sign. Then the bats came.

The following morning when I get up, the heat has already reached the mid-nineties. I decide to do some exploring before we head north again. I enter the mixed grove of eucalyptus and palms from which the bats had come, to examine the hot spring. The spring is actually part of a river which erupts from a hole—or, more precisely, a cavern. The water flows pure and clear at body temperature from the inner workings of the earth, widens into a pool about twenty feet wide by forty feet long, then, after dropping off into a short falls, flows away into the grove. I take a path deeper into the glade, the sweet sounds of rushing water helping to lower the heat a psychological degree.

The soil under the canopy is dry on the surface, but a river is flowing through the subterranean plumbing below and the roots of the plant community are tapping it. Some of the trees are enormous, more than a hundred feet high. However, there is a fundamental difference between the shade of this palm-and-eucalyptus grove and, say, the North American deciduous forest. Most trees in other parts of the world hold their leaves flat to the sun so the rays strike the surface at the perpendicular; light is a precious commodity and each leaf strives to capture as much of it as possible. In this arid Australian desert, however, there is too much light and usually there is too little water, and so the entire eucalyptus family has evolved leaves that hang downward. This allows the leaves to shed excess energy and permits the light to filter through to the ground. It also allows one to see deeper into the canopy than would be possible in a deciduous woods.

Small palms and low shrubs grow on the forest floor, nurtured by the filtered light. The foliage on this shrubbery is dotted and streaked with a dark, grainy substance that apparently arrived in liquid form and stuck to the leaves as it dried. A musky odor hangs in the air, and odd squeaks and shrieks seem to emanate from the high canopy itself.

Something moves among the leaves seventy feet above the ground. Twenty feet away from it something else moves. Then a pair of wings seem to grow out of a large, dark, hanging object. They spread wide, flap a few times, then fold back into the object. I raise my binoculars and see what appears to be a small black fox suspended upside down from the branch. It has large brown eyes, a long pointed nose, pointed ears—all aimed directly at me. Again the wings seem to sprout from its shoulders. The sunlight illuminates them from above and behind, making them glow pinkish brown. Long dark bones and red arteries taper toward the edges of the translucent fabric and stand out against the background color. He is introducing himself to me: fruit bat *Pteropus scapulatus*. Welcome to my world, he is saying. Welcome to the real world of a bat. Several feet away another one opens its wings, then another on the branch above. They all seem to be greeting me.

With a start I realize just how many are tucked away here and there in the trees. They are hanging in pairs or threesomes from the eucalyptus branches and from the bases of palm fronds. They cling to the trunks of trees, heads laid on bumps that have been conscripted for use as pillows. Some hang in groups, their wings folded around each other like football players in a huddle—except they are huddling upside down, and they look more companionable than football players, as if they are huddled merely for the pleasure of it.

Thousands of these furry upside-down creatures all looking down at me, all aiming at me with their ears and their noses. The thought occurs that the odor permeating the atmosphere is guano and the wisdom of looking up is to be questioned; but I am wearing glasses, and my mouth is firmly closed, as it should be.

However, I cannot help gazing upward. The sight is too fascinating, particularly as the details of daily life begin to play themselves out. I look back at the first bat, and as he gazes down on me he lets go of his branch with one foot and, twisting in the air, scratches his ear in a blur of gouging blows, exactly like a cat or dog. Clearly he is a male, for his testicles cannot be overlooked. They are enormous and, unlike the rest of his body, almost naked.

In many of the smaller mammals, the testes reside in the body cavity for most of the year and descend into the scrotal sac only during the breeding season, when sperm are produced. Sperm are exceedingly sensitive to high temperatures, and the scrotum deals with this fact by expanding and contracting, suspending the testes at an appropriate distance from the body's heat. Should the temperature of the air drop too low for the good of the sperm, the testes ascend into the body cavity and the scrotum shrinks into a small, wrinkled wad of skin. Fruit bats are unusual in that the testes travel the full circuit from the scrotal hammock to the body cavity on a daily basis throughout the year, not just during the breeding time.

Everywhere the trees are filled with bats hanging from eucalyptan rafters and attending to their toilette. Their priorities are clear: wings first, body second. Fastidiously, meticulously, indefatigably, they lick and groom their wings. Wings mean life. They must be kept in the best possible repair, washed, oiled, and carefully folded away. (When their body temperature reaches about 105°F, these bats lick their wings and necks for another reason: to deposit saliva. This evaporates, exactly as sweat evaporates, and carries off heat from the body.)

A shaft of sunlight levers its way over the leaves that have been shading my little friend and now falls on his "hang" ("perch" does not describe the foothold of a roosting bat). He responds by fanning himself. With his wings enfolding his body in the fashion of Dracula, he ventilates by patting his chest—like a woman fluttering her dress on a hot day. Throughout the forest, bats hanging in shafts of sunlight are ventilating in the same way. A surprising number are leaving their hangs and flying around the trees, apparently to find a better roosting spot. On takeoff, they flap their wings but continue to hold on to the branch with their feet; the lift raises their bodies parallel to the ground, and only then do they loosen their grip and fly away.

One comes floating in my direction, which means that it is also approaching the bat I have been watching. When the flier gets within three or four feet, the first emits a loud shriek. There's not much doubt about his meaning. The bats are becoming territorial in preparation for breeding, and even though the territory may be no larger than a palm frond in four to six feet of airspace, it is still a territory and is essential for attracting a female. The squabbling is constant, a shrill treble that plays over the rushing bass of the nearby waterfall, a vaudeville of downright, downstanding bats.

It is also an upside-down society, and I use the word "society" with confidence and respect. This particular species, *Pteropus scapulatus*, has a well-studied relative, *Pteropus alecto*, that boasts a social structure like a human town. The bats congregate in giant camps during the Australian spring and summer, September through March. The females, which have conceived during the previous mating season, now give birth while hanging by their toes, and then settle down to the work of rearing their infants.

For the first three weeks the females carry their infants with them as they forage for food. The young cling to their mothers with special claws designed to snag her fur, and special recurved milk teeth that grasp the teat in an unshakable grip. But after the third week the mothers deposit their infants in "night camps"—communal roosts

in well-foliated trees—and fly away on their own to gather food
throughout the night. When the mothers return the next morning
they call to their young. The young call back. The mother lands; an
infant scrambles over to her. The mother smells its chest, for three-
week-old infants cannot recognize their mothers and will try to
board anyone. If her own, she pulls back her wings, exposing her
breast, and the infant clambers on. She gives it a vigorous washing
with her tongue, then, in the most maternal gesture of the natural
world, she enfolds it in her wings. It nurses and falls asleep, swaddled
in warm, soft membrane.

At about four months the offspring begin to leave their mothers
and join packs of up to fifty juvenile bats associated with fifteen or so
adults, most of which are males. The adults act as mentors and teach
the methods and conventions of aggression and such social graces as
mutual grooming.

Meanwhile the mature males are beginning to defend territories.
The females, their offspring now on their own, will soon become
sexually receptive, and to win a mate, a male will have to own property.

When the territorial acquisitions and mate selections have more
or less stabilized, the camp has become stratified into the bat's equivalent of social classes. Around the perimeter live the males who
have not succeeded in establishing a place of their own. These dis-
enfranchised losers function as guards and alert the camp to intru-
sions. Inside the circle of lower-class bats lies the equivalent of
the middle class. These are known as "family groups" and consist
of a male, a female, and the female's offspring conceived the previous season. These males are always monogamous—good, strong,
middle-class values—and defend their territories staunchly. Then
inside the middle-class family neighborhood there lie the "adult
groups," led by truly aggressive males who, like the tycoons of the
human world, acquire things. They have acquired territory in the

choicest area: the center of the camp. They often take several females to mate, and the females are not burdened by offspring from
the previous season.

Such generalized facts of fruit-bat existence run through my
mind like a voice-over commentary, the legacy of my many years as
a student. Up above, the real-life documentary is projecting itself
across the canopy and the academic voice soon trails off. No reality
on earth quite compares with the daily trials of the fruit bat, and
even the way the creatures move rivets the mind.

Sometimes the bats grasp the branches with their wrists, which
are armed with claws, as well as with their hind feet, which also have
claws, and scramble along the boughs upside down. Sometimes they
travel between boughs by traversing the tree trunk. They spread
their wings, grasp as much of the trunk as they can, secure a grip
with their claws, and lunge upward with their hind legs. Grasping
the new position with their wrist claws, they can draw their legs up
under the rump for the next upward lunge. They progress this way
like little lumberjacks with climbing spikes, until they reach their
destination. And sometimes they simply sidle along the branches
while hanging upside down, sliding the lead leg out from the body to
the right or left and drawing the opposite leg after. The object of
these movements seems almost invariably to be aggression. They
are always probing the territorial boundaries, always testing the
neighbor's mettle. The neighbors, on the other hand, are always
willing to defend themselves, and they rush toward the aggressors in
a vigorous, sideways charge, which culminates in a shriek. If the
shriek is not enough, a series of blows usually is, the contestants
hanging upside down and buffeting each other about the head with
their folded wings.

An etiquette underlies these contests, conventions of aggression, which the bats learn as juveniles. Aggression has to be controlled and channeled. If not, it becomes so dangerous that it can-

cels the benefits of living in a social group. It negates the defensive strength of numbers, the power of cooperative effort.

Social benefits do not come cheap. When any creature joins a society it loses personal freedom and accepts the responsibility of self-restraint. It is thrown into competition with its peers and is forced to fight for position in a peck order. However, if the cost of membership becomes so inflated that it exceeds the cost of living singly, there is no point to social life—why worry about eagles or snakes if your immediate neighbor is more dangerous?—and your evolution will probably lead back to the solitary life.

The minds of fruit bats have been designed to avoid such dire costs and to maintain a beneficial balance. And so the squabbles resolve themselves with negotiated boundaries or with one of the contestants flying off to find a more tranquil spot among the branches and leaves. The activity goes on throughout the day, for these bats, with their excellent eyesight, are well equipped for coping with light.

Here comes one now. There is a gap between two gnarled, ancient eucalypts, and into this bight surge the waves of solar energy. An equally ancient and magnificent palm, having laid claim to this photosynthetic feast, has thrust itself into the opening. And toward the palm flies a bat that has probably been dispossessed from somewhere nearby. It flies with that wonderful shambling flight made possible by the elastic membranes of the chiropteran wing. Membranes stretch between the long, graceful fingers at the tip of the wing and connect along the side of the body between the arm and the front edge of the hind leg. By pulling the leg backward or pushing it forward the bat can adjust the membrane's tension. A network of fine muscles in the membrane itself and numerous small tendons allow even finer adjustments as the wing caresses the air.

The bat glides in slowly and circles the palm once, twice, three times, head turning left, right, tilting up, down, sizing up the situation. The tree is a species of fan palm; its fronds consist of a long shaft, three or four feet long, with the leaf itself fanning out at the end. As with all palms, the fronds begin by sprouting up from the center of the trunk. As they mature the leaf opens, and the entire frond gradually droops lower as younger fronds take its place at top and center. Finally, toward the end of its life, the frond sags down at a shallow angle to the palm trunk, eventually dies, and assumes its position flat against the trunk in a kind of dead-frond skirt; the crown, meanwhile, grows ever higher, leaving the dead fronds fastened in place farther and farther below.

One of these older fronds is hanging down at about a thirty degree angle to the trunk, and the new arrival decides on the fourth pass that this is where he wants to land. He comes in carefully, reaches out with his hind feet as he passes by, and snags the shaft of the frond about two feet below its attachment to the tree. Another frond hangs down in the same position about a foot away. The bat grabs this with its wing claws.

And there he hangs. But apparently it is not the position he had intended. You can see him assess the situation. His head scans the nearby palm trunk. If I could just reach over and grab the trunk I could cling to it for the day . . . what a great roost that would be . . . but I don't know if I can. . . .

And he reaches out with his right hind. It's just a little . . . too . . . far . . . but . . . uhhhn! And with a last, millimetric lunge he manages to catch a claw on the tree trunk. Now, though, he is suspended like a hammock, belly to the sky, between the palm frond and the tree trunk. With his left wing clutching the frond, his right toenails clinging to the bark, he reaches toward the trunk with his other foot. But he can't come close. He is beginning to get irritated and frustrated.

He stretches his right wing toward the trunk, but it is a tentative gesture, a feeble expression of a weak idea rather than a bona fide attempt. It comes across as mime. Ah, Marcel, for surely that's what your name must be, in your furry hide, with your skin-draped wings, from your preposterous position in the sky, you are playing out the absurd workings of the mind. Clearly, the situation now calls for a drastic maneuver. The pointed nose and the large brown eyes peer back between the legs and scan the palm up and down; his head tilts back 180 degrees until it is craned straight out, like a man looking to heaven for God, and the nose and the eyes and the ears examine the palm fronds. The mind is calculating: Fronds here by head, tree beyond feet . . .

He makes his move. Wings flop, legs extend, dangle and retract—it's hard to tell at first just what exactly he hopes to accomplish, but you get the impression he is trying to crawl over himself—and finally he succeeds!

But no—he is *still* suspended like a hammock between the trunk and the fronds. He has merely rotated his predicament. Now his head points toward the palm trunk, his right wing clings to a bump on the tree, and his left leg grasps one of the fronds. After all that effort, all that motion, all he has managed to do is reverse his position. What a superb politician he would make.

As if he can read my thoughts (or maybe he has noticed my hoots of derision), he turns and looks down at me, past his wingpit.

No more finesse. Clever solutions have had their chance. With his belly still facing the sky and his body swaying in the breeze, he looks along his underside at the palm frond grasped in his left foot. He lunges toward it—a desperate, flopping leap over himself. He reaches out with both wings and clutches at the frond's shaft, at the same time retaining the original grip with both feet. He ends up clinging to the frond with his entire body.

The shaft, however, is smooth and slick, and despite his clutching grip he begins to slide, slowly, gradually, but ineluctably, down, down, down, to the palm leaf terminating the shaft. He looks down helplessly, looks up yearningly, but, like a fire fighter down the firehouse pole, he slides until he hits the leaf. There he comes to a halt.

He is now holding on to the upper edges of the leaf fan by the hooks on his thumbs (thumbs that look like wrists from our human point of view). And, fortunately, it is not such a bad place to end up. He finds himself on the south side of the leaf, shielded from the sun. All around him thousands of competitive, aggressive bats who have won their daily roosting places are fanning themsleves because the sun has changed position and is dousing them with radiant energy. A few of them are probably behind the travails of my little friend. But he is stretched out against the sky, swiveling his furry head around to reconnoiter his good fortune.

There is nothing cryptic in any of this, no particular message. Except to say that those who think that animals don't think, those who think that animals cannot think because they cannot speak human words—well, I do not have much time for those disconnected people. They have lost touch with the intuitive truth of things. I do not know what the thoughts of a fruit bat are like because his language is incomprehensible to me. But looking up at Marcel looking down on me, I know how his feelings feel.

They feel exactly the way my own feelings felt when, as a teenage boy, I attempted to scale a large rock in the desert. Engrossed in reaching the top, I lost sight of reality and discovered by and by that not only was the surface too steep to climb higher, but it was also too steep to risk descending. I was not thinking in nouns and verbs, "My God, I am caught on a rock in a high place!" I simply knew on some deep, cellular level that I was suspended. I was knowing the truths and realities that faced me, not thinking them. Eventually the mind figured a way out, but it was not a matter of rational thought. I simply feared my way down from that rock, millimeter by terrifying millimeter.

So it is with a sense of kinship that I gaze up at my little friend, a kinship that one should feel, in the compulsive pursuit of one's own life, with all things living, striving, and dying.

But the time has come to push on to Darwin, Australia's northernmost city, and again seek the company of my own species. I am not sure I appreciate the prospect. As the bat peers down, it occurs to me that standing at this point on the globe I, too, am hanging upside down with respect to my friends on the northern half of the sphere. The bat, from their point of view, is actually the upright individual. I look up one last time and chuckle at the ironies.

DIVORCE

AMONG THE

GULLS

It's a nice day on the Farallon Islands. The sun is out. The 50°F wind is only relentless, not vicious. It's similar, all things considered, to a good day in San Francisco, twenty miles to the east.

The local residents are soaking up the glad ambience. They've settled into a more or less even pattern by laying claim to little pieces of rocky real estate: nesting territories. These are Western gulls, and the subdivisions create a neighborly regularity. The regularity is not the only semblance of neighborhood, though. A lazy chorus of mewlings, yelps, "laughs," and "keks" rises from the colony, indicating the invisible web of competitive tension that unifies the individuals into a social system, into a living, interacting *thing*. Each gull eyes the tidbits of grass and pebble on its neighbor's plot, each gull beams avarice and envy toward that which is not his or hers, each gull gleams defiance at the implied intentions of its neighbors—just a nice day on the home front, the cries and yelps of domestic bliss mingling in a sort of twelve-tone avian Muzak.

A large male sits quietly on his own grass-on-rock nest, his white head and neck contrasting smartly with his black back. Occasionally he nibbles at a stone or a stray blade of grass, then nods off in the sun with his breast pressed warmly against three freckled, buff-brown eggs. Tranquility, however, is not long for his world. A series of loud, almost catlike wails breaks forth overhead, and a second gull, his mate, glides in for a landing with the exuberant familiarity of someone who belongs and is emphasizing the fact that "I have arrived." It is apparent that what we are about to witness is a private matter.

It so happens, however, that the scene is being watched by a human female, a biologist named Judith Hand. She sits in a small shack about six feet away, armed with a tape recorder, binoculars, and a notebook. She wears a parka in order to endure the wind driving through the cracks in the walls, has been here since dawn, and will remain until dusk. Her purpose? To record every action, every sound, every intention that the seventeen pairs in this immediate area make public in the course of nesting.

The scene continues. The female picks up a few leaves of dried grass, walks toward her mate, and stands there, grass in beak, all the while mewling in a way that sounds plaintive to human ears. The male ignores her, sitting on the eggs without the slightest show of concern. This is not, of course, what the female wants. So she squats slightly, tilts up her rear, lowers her breast and head, pumps her neck up and down, and emits a choking, pumping sound as if she's gagging. A feeling of domestic tension now begins to build, even for a human observer.

As if realizing the cold shoulder is not going to work, the male now responds. He, too, assumes a slight crouch, and, stern up, bow down, he chokes back to his mate, but even more emphatically: He does not *want* to give up the eggs.

She stands there a moment, as if contemplating this attitude, then drops her beakful of grass, turns, and walks away.

About six minutes later, here comes the female again, more dry grass dangling from her beak (sarcasm may be ruled out as a motive, but only because she's a gull). More mewling, but this time more urgent. Another episode of choking, the male again refusing to leave. Once again the female drops her bouquet and walks away.

Six minutes later, and *again* she comes back, beak bristling with the obligatory grass, mewling with very evident determination. Now she is choking with fearsome intensity. And this time, as if he realizes the show is over, the male gets up without reply, and *he* walks away. The female stands over the nest, fluffs her breast feathers to expose the brood patch—a naked patch of skin that provides warmth directly to the eggs—and carefully settles down. As her breast presses against the warm, smooth eggs she shakes her tail and tilts her head up, giving the impression that nothing in this world is so infinitely pleasurable as brooding one's eggs, which for a seagull is probably true. It is worth a confrontation with one's mate.

To Judith Hand, there is much more going on here than a simple squabble over the changing of the guard. Under normal circumstances, as the group members compete for food or nesting plots or mates, the bigger, the stronger, the more determined individuals win and eventually establish dominance. (In many animals, dominance is worked out during childhood in that same rough-and-tumble play that to us seems simple, pure fun.) This sets up the peck order, in which the top individual can take what it wants, when it wants, with little more than a few threatening gestures. Subordinates back down. In the grand overview of life, dominance ensures that the strongest survive and pass on their genes, even when times are hard.

It goes without saying, though, that in its extreme forms, dominance can lead to harsh, tyrannical systems which allow little hope for the weak. Not surprisingly, most humans find the whole idea of dominance and submission vaguely unsettling, as if recognizing that there but for the grace of God go I. We will not go into the mat-

ter of God's graces, but keep in mind that despots, godfathers, tycoons, and so forth all fit the classical mold of the arch-dominant
male. Many political systems are based on the bald, unrepentant
dominance that is sometimes described as tyranny. And if it seems
like a long leap from the seagulls' little plot on the Farallon Islands
to the capitals of Russia and America, keep the principles of dominance clearly in mind.

However, the little drama we have just witnessed underscores a
remarkable variation on the theme of dominance: the mated pair
have worked out their differences through a battle of wills, not physical combat. Standard dominance and submission are obviously not
in operation. It turns out that when these gulls pair off to mate and
raise a family, a radically different set of standards takes over, a set
designed to accommodate the wants and needs of both partners.
Furthermore, it is based on a complex language of postures and calls,
communication in the truest sense. The "choking" is actually a ritualized display which revealed, after three bouts, that the female
would not be denied.

Judith Hand has termed this whole system of conflict resolution
"egalitarianism." In contrast to pure dominance, in which the dominant individual wins nearly 100 percent of the time, in egalitarian
relationships each of the two parties wins roughly 50 percent of the
time. This is true for the two gulls. Choking therefore works both
ways, and there are many times when the male "persuades" his mate
to relinquish the eggs so he, too, can have his share of the domestic
pleasures. Somehow it's comforting to know that egalitarian systems have evolved naturally in the wild, that there is a natural al-
ternative to Might Makes Right, that the egalitarian way is not
some flimsy artifice which humans cling to in order to deny the truth
of reality. That maybe egalitarianism is a strong, natural choice.

There is an intriguing aside to equality among the gulls, and it has to
do with what can only be called divorce. Like humans, many gull

species are described as monogamous: they're supposed to mate for life. So much for suppositions. It turns out that, depending on the species and the location, more than 25 percent of young, newly paired gulls split up after their first attempt at raising a family.

How could gulls possibly be incompatible? What conceivable grounds could threaten their bond? According to Judith Hand, it comes down to a matter of basic temperament and emotional constitution. Suppose, for example, that the male is a domestic sort and he wants to incubate 70 percent of the time; suppose that the female, too, craves the pleasures of nesting and she also wants to incubate 70 percent of the time. Turning to the rules of egalitarian behavior, they spend 40 percent of their time squabbling, and this can have dire consequences. If the strife becomes sufficiently acrimonious, eggs can be crushed and chicks can be injured. Foraging time is cut down and the chicks can be undernourished. And if the conflict prevents the chicks from fledging, that is grounds for divorce. The pair show up the next year with new mates. Rarely does the new partner want to incubate more than 30 percent of the time.

Divorce among the gulls gives some interesting insights to divorce among *Homo sapiens*. It shows, for example, that there is such a thing as fundamental incompatibility. Gulls cannot make excuses. For them, incompatibility is based on the bedrock of basic psycho-biological differences. Childhood trauma, permissive parents, dominant siblings, nosy in-laws, hair in the sink, toilet paper rolled underhand versus overhand—these are reasons fabricated by the rationalizing mind to disguise the deeper, truer reasons, which are emotional differences.

Of course, the human mind is capable of convincing itself that black is white and white is black, and, given the ambience of modern society, that petty differences represent insurmountable incompatibilities. How does one differentiate between the insignificant and the fundamental? It is not an easy task, especially when people are young and have little experience. At that point, what is actually an insignificant slight in the big scheme of life can seem like a monumental obstruction in the little scheme of the moment. This is probably the reason that the marriage vow is phrased as it is, "Till death do you part." If taken seriously, it will help distinguish the trivial from the significant, for it encourages a couple to give matrimony their most persistent effort (I was going to say "shot," but reconsidered). It pushes them past the abrasive trivialities. What is left is the fundamental stuff.

What constitutes a fundamental difference between human mates, a true reason to call the marriage quits? If the gulls offer any guidance, you would have to say that a true incompatibility—one that all of nature would accept as grounds for divorce—threatens the family or the lives of its members. Mutual brawling, death threats, attempted suicide, battery and sexual abuse, deep depression—these would drive any normal gull to divorce. They are biological grounds. They cast a new light on the marriage vow, which ought to be amended, "Till (attempted) death do you part."

It is now four and a half hours later, and the female is still incubating. But sitting there imparting heat is no longer the pleasure it once was. A normal sitting lasts about three hours, and she has already had to leave the nest briefly to relieve herself. Hunger is also making demands, and why doesn't the male get his brood patch back here so she can leave?

Finally, an obstreperous call blasts out overhead—*he* has arrived—and this time there is no dawdling around with tufts of grass and emotional paraphernalia. The female gets up immediately and walks away from the eggs. Without delay the male waddles over to the nest and settles down. The two are in full agreement, so no further communication is necessary. It makes you think of Oscar Wilde's immortal comment on relationships: "If two people get along perfectly . . . one of them is . . . unnecessary." The male, whose eyes are closing in ecstasy at the feel of the warm, round eggs, would agree. The female, who is flying off hungrily, angrily, in search of food, would not.

MEMBERSHIP

IN THE

PIGEON

CLUB

I stood at the end of the Dana Point pier and looked out, not at the open sea, as you would expect from such a vantage point, but at a restaurant. It rested about seventy meters offshore on an island manufactured from Honda-sized rocks, and both pier and restaurant stood in the stagnant backwaters of a modern marina.

It is a typical Southern California harbor: A forest of aluminum masts bristles over the marina proper, a strange, naked, dull-metal winter of a scene. Set back from the slips sits a cluster of hotels, restaurants, and gift shops, all designed by the same architect in a fusion of styles—Cape Cod-California Ranch—California Cod, for lack of a formal tag. Bikinied women, young and outrageous, and gray-haired, Hawaiian-shirted men with large bellies and rubber sandals meander in and out of these shops and restaurants, bored beyond comprehension, idly searching for meaningful trinkets and memorabilia, narcotized by this predictable, completely altered world. A world designed for habit without exertion—not a boulder in the path, not a bush or tree diverting the concrete walkways, not a meter from the parking lot to the buildings.

The land surrounding this architectural dream has been smothered with asphalt, and alien plants from desert climates (eucalyptus and palms) have been imported to give the *illusion* of nature. But these plants are not suited to brine air and salted sand, and their leaves are turning brown and dropping; or their fronds are dying back at the ends and fraying. Sod has been patched and quilted in thick, rubbery sheets around some of the buildings, but has developed a nutritional deficiency and come down with big yellow blotches. It has been laid over a soil of decomposed sandstone. A cactus might have a chance here; not grass.

The harbor is fabricated, too. A thin line of breakwater rock has been built from the side of Dana Point and trails south for about a mile, shielding the beach from the world-wrapping immensity of the Pacific Ocean.

I had spent many days here as a boy twenty-five years before, fishing over this same scarred rail, and as I stood there looking out at the restaurant and the breakwater beyond, my vision adjusted. I was looking out into the past.

I am standing on a cliff. The salt wind blows against my face, cold and stinging, and I gaze down on as wonderful a scene as nature ever devised. Nestled against the base of Dana Point itself lies a small cove. To the south lie several smaller coves, each with a crescent beach of yellow sand walled off from the next cove by a tongue of rocks protruding into the sea. It is a private, isolated world, lodged between the ocean and the naked, rugged cliffs, for no roads have snaked into it.

The memory shifts. Now I am down on the beach looking up. I have just read *Two Years Before the Mast*, Richard Henry Dana's classic account of life along the California coast two hundred years ago. I stare at those same sandstone cliffs that Dana described, admire the same pebbles and fossilized shells embedded there. There is Dana himself, laboring as an ordinary seaman alongside Mexican workers in their white tunics and baggy white pantaloons. They roll bundles of oxhides over the edge, bundles that kick up clouds of dust and showers of pebbles as they bound down the cliff. Here on the beach, other sailors load the hides into wooden dories, then row the cargo out to the ship anchored in the cove.

Now I am walking along the beach of the next cove south. Great soggy brown piles of kelp lie strewn about, stranded by the tide. There is a dead sea lion, an old male as big as an ox, scarred and worn and now dissolving back into the earth. Seagulls balance on its carcass, pecking at the eyes. Sandpipers skitter along the line of foam that advances and retreats with each new wave, and pelicans bob on the water behind the breakers.

Beyond the pelicans, the waves, after days of relentlessly slipping through the sea, approach the shore. Several hundred yards out each rises ominously in its turn to embrace the black, mussel-crusted rocks that stand guard at the mouth of each cove. As the walls of water glide forward, the rocks seemed to rise and fall, like the teeth of a giant jaw, frothing while the monster chews. Reduced to swells, the once magnificent waves wallow meekly toward shore, rocking the pelicans and gulls that reflect quietly on the surface. The energy that has pushed mountains of water for ten thousand miles slides onto the beach and, finally exhausted, leaves the water flat on the sand.

The coves, the foaming rocks, the kelp, the sea lions—they are long gone. I stood there on the pier looking at the changes we have wrought, and I thought for a moment about the nature of change. The truth is, change is the order of things and always has been. Ice spreads from the poles, drapes over the globe, then shrinks back. It advances and recedes, advances and recedes, in the metronomic beat of the ages. Lava belches from the innards of the earth, cyclones and floods lash its surface like static through the uncountable seasons, meteors punctuate the eons with cataclysm. These are formidable, often devastating events, but they are also standard events.

The basic challenge of life, against which all living things are aligned, is coping with change. Life must adapt. If it succeeds in the long term, the adaptation is called evolution. I was reminded of this fundamental fact by a rustling, pattering noise at my feet. Looking down, I saw that I had been surrounded by pigeons.

There are few creatures more opportunistic than the pigeon. In a few short decades it has taken advantage of the tarmac and the sidewalks and the gutters of its human hosts. It has moved into the rafters and turrets that hark back to the nooks and crannies of its native cliffs. It has switched to a diet of crumbs and crusts that approximates, in a decidedly inferior way, the nutritional value of its ancestral seeds. The pigeon has even changed its coat and taken up a fashion of sooty grays splattered with blotches of off-white in order to blend with the paper-on-tar of its new niche.

They clustered there beneath me, a seething mass of bag birds drawn compulsively to a creature that their minds had come to tolerate and to associate with food, their little red, round, pinhole-pupiled eyes glinting like sequins with instinctive expectations. Poised for that instant when my hand might fling some scrap their way, they craned their necks; but their racial memory kept them alert to the fact that what I threw might be a rock. The conflict came out in that fitful tic of a gait peculiar to pigeons, heads jerking back and forth in syncopated beat with their pink feet, and all the while hunger and the competitive urge push, pull, against apprehension.

A crumpled bag with several crusts was lying nearby, so I broke off a small piece and tossed it to the left. Twenty-five or thirty pigeons stampeded the left, feet pattering like rain on the deck. They jostled for position, shouldering each other aside, and pelted the planks with their beaks. I tossed some crumbs to the right. The twenty-five or thirty scrambled to the right. Twenty-five or thirty of these graceless, practical creatures rubbed and shoved for position long after the crumbs had disappeared into a few lucky gullets. It was then that a revelation occurred. Evolution itself appeared before me, in the form of a willet.

He—I use the masculine because . . . well . . . because it just *seemed* like a male. It could have been a female, because most shorebirds are dressed in perfectly unisexual patterns and cannot be told apart visually. But to my mind, on that day, fixing on English airs, it had to be a male.

He dressed with impeccable, conservative taste in subdued grays and beige. His monocle—the eye he trained on me the way birds often do—was a light, shining brown. His dapper gray back was a walking coat, his long, elegant legs his boots. He walked straight into the jostling rabble of pigeons with a slow, graceful stride.

The fact that he was among the pigeons at all was astonishing. Willets are citizens of the sandy beaches and the shoreline rocks where pigeons never go. What was going on? Birds, with their incredibly high metabolism and small, heat-releasing bodies cannot afford to waste time dallying. One like this probably had a body temperature of over $100°F$ ($37.8°C$), and his corpse would be as cold as the air within a half hour of dying. He would have to be hustling food continuously; and he did indeed appear to be looking.

But for what? Willets are predators. They use their three-inch bills to probe for worms and crustaceans that live in the intertidal sand. Their stomachs are designed for animal protein. What edible thing could a willet possibly find on the dry, splintery deck of an old pier?

Then came the next revelation. As the pigeons continued to jostle and shove and neurotically peck the planks, the willet cocked his head to eye some object. Ever graceful, he bowed down and slipped his bill into the crack between two planks, then lifted his head, and there, grasped delicately in the tips of his bill, was half a Twinkie. Tilting his head back, he gave two quick gulps, and the Twinkie was gone. A lump moved down his neck and disappeared in his breast.

Clearly, this was no ordinary willet, and unless pigeons had kidnapped him as a young chick, the explanation for his behavior would have to be genetic, as evolution always is. Here was another wild creature whose traditional habitat was making way for development. Dana Point, like all of Orange County, was being paved down to the sea and, in the case of the launching ramps, into it— and so, like all the creatures whose world was being obliterated, the species willet had the evolutionary choice of adapting to the new environment, as the pigeons had done, or going extinct. The individual before me might be that first magical step in adapting, that chance in ten million, one hundred million (the odds are infinite), in which mutation lands on some winning combination, on some odd constellation of behaviors that just happens to work and launches the creature into a revolutionary style of life.

The signs of uniqueness were not difficult to discern. For one, this individual was far calmer than a normal willet: A typical self-respecting willet would never stand nonchalantly four feet from a human being, on a pier, surrounded by pigeons. Very likely his temperament was calmer than normal, and temperament is subject to the laws of inheritance. The odds were, this bird before me was a sport that through the quirks of genetic chance had ended up on the verge of a brave new world. If he could find a mate he might become a sort of father of his country and sire a whole new line.

True, any new line descended from this bird needed a lot of improvement before it joined the select company of the pigeon. This became abundantly clear as I watched my unorthodox friend stalk slowly and gracefully among the drab, agitating rabble, peering into the cracks between the planks. Since the pigeons could not reach there with their stubby beaks, he had virtually no competition. But he also had no discrimination. Again he probed deep into a crack, coming up with a Band-Aid, complete with wrapper.

"No," I thought, "He's not going to—"

Three gulps were needed to get it down, but down it went, a rectangular lump sliding down my willet's neck to its destiny with the Twinkie. But that's the thing about evolution. It's not supposed to start out perfect. The important thing is the breakthrough, the toehold on a new niche. There's plenty of time later for calibration and fine adjustments.

I turned toward the sea again—the restaurant, actually—to contemplate these notions. Several minutes later children's footsteps came pounding out onto the pier.

"Over there—birds!" shouted a little voice, reveling in the novelty of creatures that were actually wild.

"What's that skinny thing!?" shouted another little voice.

"I dunno—maybe it's a baby pelican . . . ?" answered the first, obviously referring to the willet, as no pelicans could be seen.

"I wonder if there's anything wrong with it?" shouted the first little voice, and I turned around just in time to see a boy of about ten charging the flock, arms whirling like helicopter blades, followed by his younger brother, a lad of about nine. With their civilized temperaments, the birds held their ground much longer than wild pigeons or normal willets would, but the gyrating boys were more than even they could handle. With a great clapping of wings and a loud whoosh of battered air, the flock leaped into the sky.

"Nope. It flies okay," announced the first boy to the second, while the 25 or 30 pigeons and the one willet circled out over the marina.

A very heavy woman, obviously the children's mother, came puffing onto the pier, and I turned away to face the restaurant again, the two kids now having gotten down on all fours in order to explore between the planks with grubby little fingers. Each species to its own, I thought. Fragments of my own boyhood flashed before my eyes.

"Ma, Ma! Look! *Real sea life!*" Ecstasy bordering on hysteria. I turned to see this real life and saw the older boy running over to show his mother what appeared to be a Tootsie Roll. Looking closer, I realized it was a dried clam—bait that had fallen between the planks. And then it struck me why the willet had come. A clam, dry or wet, was the kind of morsel a willet could digest. It was the kind of small item that fishermen lost between the cracks and didn't bother to recover.

I turned again toward the restaurant, the memories of my youth forever altered, just as the pigeons and the willet set their wings and came gliding in for a landing. The wind whistled through their feathers as they banked and settled down, each engineering itself onto a precisely targeted spot. I shivered as I realized what a wonderful thing evolution really is.

NEW EDEN,
CITY OF
BEASTS

From time to time the advertising and journalistic media refer to New York as the Big Apple. It's a loaded metaphor. Slyly arrogant, it is a sort of oxymoronic gambit that pokes fun at the city by comparing it with a pome; it also aggrandizes, hinting at the sheer immensity of the cultural fruit. It beckons, challenges: the Mecca of Western civilization. Come in from Hicksville and be amazed. Brush that straw off your pants. Kick that manure off your boots. See what man hath made of the biblical Garden. Take a bite of the *Big Apple.*

"Big Apple" says all of that. The science, the technology, the attitude of human centrality, the philosophies, the religions, the arts are all implied. But there is one symbolism here that goes untrumpeted. Standing as it does for a sensational maze of glass and reinforced concrete, representing the almost total burial of an island beneath human constructions, Big Apple represents that which is strange to nature and alien to all but a few species of creature.

Well, with all this symbolism packed into one huge fruit, it was inevitable that the second largest city in America would want to compete. The inevitable happened in 1977 when a magazine known as *New West* referred to Los Angeles as the "Big Avocado." Like "Big Apple," the term "Big Avocado" contained all the self-aggrandizing symbols of human achievement. It also hinted at the particular features that draw humans to this city, including the climate and the exotic nature of the ornamental shrubbery, for avo-cados actually grow in Los Angeles as surely as apples do not in New York.

But in addition to all that, "Big Avocado" contained symbolism that the magazine completely overlooked. The giant berries, which is technically what avocados are, represent a fabulous source of food to anyone observant, nimble, and determined enough to partake of the harvest. Such beings did in fact exist. Los Angeles, the Big Avocado, was obliviously supplying a large and growing population of rats, opossums, coyotes, raccoons, skunks, foxes, squirrels, pigeons, starlings, cockroaches, snails, and other wild animals with real avocados, the big berry.

Unlike New York, which has been built up vertically, Los Angeles has spread out horizontally in a single layer of homes. The land has not been as thoroughly coated with asphalt and cement, and bushes and trees thrive in the small patches of exposed earth. An enormous number of homes have yards in front and behind, and a significant percentage of these use avocado trees for landscaping and casual harvest. Tens, maybe hundreds of thousands of these trees grow in backyards throughout the Los Angeles conurbation. And the avocado is one of the most sophisticated, nutritious foods on the market. It contains about 4 percent protein—extremely high for a fruit—55 to 60 percent fat, and a wide range of vitamins and minerals. During the ripening season, hundreds of pounds of avocados may fall to the ground under a large tree, where they are often available to coyotes, rats, skunks, foxes, raccoons, and many other animals for months on end. Omnivores, animals that eat all, can grow fat indeed on an avocado diet.

But, common as they are, avocados account for just a fraction of the available food in greater Los Angeles. When you consider the hundreds of other fruit, nut, and vegetable species that also grow there; when you throw in the tons and tons of perfectly nutritious garbage from several million households and countless restaurants; when you factor in the food that small creatures such as rats, mice, and cockroaches have access to before it even becomes garbage — when you consider all that, what you have is a bounteous source of life.

What animal would not want its share? And although it is true that as human habitation spreads, it annexes the habitat of other species, development can be beneficial: It creates ledges and parks for nesting, nooks and crannies for shelter, territories for food and breeding, all free for the taking. *If* you can live with the people. Or if you can live *despite* the people. Not every animal has what it takes to survive in the human heartland. Urban existence requires a special combination of size, diet, temperament, and habits.

There seem to be two basic ways of making it in the city. One is the humans' way: You can get domesticated. Essentially, you come to the humans and say: "I would like to live with you." The humans look you up and down, calculate your potential use, and reply: "All right. We could go for that. Here's the deal. We'll feed you and protect you and provide you with shelter. But *we'll* decide what you eat. *We'll* decide when you eat, and where you eat it. And here's the clincher. *We* will take total control of your genes. We demand the right to alter your shape, size, coat, and color, and especially your behavior and temperament, for whatever suits our purpose. Take it or leave it."

Despite the Faustian terms, the deal does have its attractions. Some animals have therefore taken the domestic path—or, rather, they have taken one of several paths, each marked with a particular price.

Suppose you were considering the domestic route and had the power to test it on a trial basis. Here is how the choices would probably appear to an independent observer with its own, nonhuman interests at heart.

Consider first the path of pethood as taken by that ultimate pet, the dog. You are now a mellow, good-natured mutt who is named, say, Uriah. Your master goes shopping at the mall and returns an hour and a half later. You are overjoyed. You are so overjoyed that you succumb to a fit of obsequious ecstasy. Your body writhes and your tail whips. You jump and lick your master's hands, whinny, yap, and whine, and sometimes you even lose control of your bladder. You cannot help yourself. Like virtually all domesticated animals, your mind has been altered to retain juvenile traits.

This can happen naturally in the course of normal evolution, where it is known as "neoteny." Neoteny is the retention of juvenile characteristics by the sexually mature adult. Newts, which are salamanders that live in water and retain their gills, are neotenic. *Homo sapiens*, which retains the less ossified skeleton and skull of the immature chimpanzee or gorilla or some ancestral species, is considered a neotenic ape. Curiosity, the foundation of science and our intellectual workings, is said by some also to be a neotenic trait.

Domestication, however, applies the principle of neoteny to human ends, and a juvenile reaction to dominance   in other words, subservience and submission—are universal qualities that all domestic creatures share. They are essential traits to living among humans on human terms. They allow you to accept training, to jump when the boss says jump, and to lie down when the boss says lie down. Thrown into the bargain is the juvenile ecstasy that completely swamps your mind when the boss comes home.

(By contrast, wild animals must grow up to become defiant and intransigent. Just as people must develop a healthy level of pride, dignity, courage, and self-respect in order to function as adults, so must wild animals. Without such traits you cannot defend yourself, not to mention win a nesting site, a mate, and a decent place in the peck order, and defend your offspring. Without adult defiance and adult intransigence there is no survival.)

Instead of becoming a pet, you might try the path of the working dog—a hunting dog, for example. Let us say, a pointer. On certain occasions you will find your body thrown into an awkward three legged stance, one foot tucked under your armpit, your head and neck craned parallel to the ground, your entire body locked into a cataleptic fit—all pointed at a bird. This is a behavioral mutation that has been bred into your brain to make you a tool for the hunt.

The same principle of genetic manipulation has been applied to the dog's body. Under the domestic contract, dogs have been stretched, compressed, inflated, weighted, reduced, denuded, insulated, dyed, patterned, and permed until now we have everything from the three-pound chihuahua to the three-hundred-pound Saint Bernard. In between are creatures such as the bulldog, an animal whose features have been fashioned out of dwarf mutations so that its muzzle is pushed up into its face, its lower jaw is cantilevered out into the space where its muzzle ought to be, and its wrists have been crammed up to its elbows so it stumps along at a dead run like an amputee.

You might not care for the pet approach. Consider, then, the scientific route and become, say, a laboratory rat. In the process of being made suitable for science, this creature has been relieved of its pigmentation: A majority are albinos with pink eyes and white fur. The creature's temperament has been bleached as bland as its coat; it will endure needles jabbed repeatedly into its flesh, and electrodes shoved relentlessly into various orifices. Even when laboratory rats do resist, their fight is nowhere near as violent as that of a wild rat. A wild rat would probably die of trauma in similar straits.

If science is not for you, you can always resort to agricultural domestication. Become a cow. The cow is the bovine answer to lobotomy. The farmer wants in this creature a brain whose basic chore is to steer the carcass from the feeding trough to the stud yard to the slaughterhouse. Anything else makes the animal burn calories, which reduces the rate of weight gain. (Actually, the ideal cow wouldn't have a brain at all; it would be a tissue culture that produces flesh in a huge, pink, continuously growing salami from which steaks and roasts could be hacked at will. A nozzle at the base would produce milk. Given enough time and the great promise of genetic engineering we will no doubt succeed in breeding such a creature.)

If all this comes across as outrageous, it is not meant to be. It is a simple statement of reality from an animal's point of view. The point is, each species is trying to forward its own interests over those of any other species that happens to be handy. Keep in mind that no matter how benign selective breeding seems, the changes serve our interests at the expense of the animal's. Specialized body shapes and behavior patterns might give the animal value, hence survival, in human society, but they also cut the animal's chances of ever again surviving on its own. Picture our pointer, for instance, setting off with a pack of ancestral wolves after a moose: "A moose! A moose!" "Jeez! We know. We know."

Clearly, domestication is not for everyone; by avoiding it, one keeps (some) control of one's destiny. This brings us to the second way of breaching the Big Avocado: on *your* terms. Become an "uninvited guest." The question is, how do you live among humans and retain your rights as an autonomous, self-determining creature? How do you live in the city, take advantage of the food and lodging, and not pay what the humans ask? Uninvited guests find ways. But first, the term "uninvited guest" needs definition.

Technically, *Escherichia coli*, the bacterium that makes the human gut its universe, is an uninvited guest. So are viruses. So are follicle mites, ensconced at the roots of our hairs, fleas, head lice, crab

lice, chigoes, tapeworms, and other parasites—not one can produce an invitation. Let us exclude them from the definition. They
are so small, in the case of the microbes, or they are so different from
us, in the case of the parasites, that it just doesn't seem proper to apply the word "guest." As I intend the term, "uninvited guest" refers
to vertebrates, to reptiles, amphibians, mammals, and birds. A few
of the insects, because of their omnipotent abilities and overwhelming presence, crawled into the definition, but most of them
have no effect on our lives.

Uninvited guests force themselves into our affairs in various
ways. Some, like the escaped parrots, draw attention with their
striking colors and strident calls. Some, like the roof rat and the
brown rat, attract notice by competing with us for food and living
space and leaving trash behind in the process. Like the raccoon and
the opossum, some uninvited guests become pests by eating food put
out for pets, or even by eating the pets themselves; they provoke us
by entering garages and attics, raiding garbage bins, dying between
our walls. On odd occasions, these creatures pose a physical threat,
biting and clawing when petted, picked up, or backed into a corner.
A greater threat is the ability of some to harbor rabies, encephalitis,
plague, and other infectious diseases.

Uninvited guests, then, are wild animals that move into our cities, draw our wrath with their habits, but retain their status as autonomous creatures and show no inclination to leave, despite our
best efforts to force them out.

To give you some idea of how successful some of these creatures
have been, the Los Angeles County Department of Animal Control received more than 3,600 complaints or "alerts" on opossums,
coyotes, skunks, and other creatures in 1988. That's an average of
ten calls per day. The calls are made because roof rats thrive in
shrubs, attics, palms, hedges, and they commute along power and
telephone cables. Opossums nest in low, dense shrubbery and walk
to their grocery outlets along backyard fences. Skunks live beneath

our houses, in our walls. Coyotes course up and down our alleys. Parrots roost in our eucalyptus trees. Crows live the good life at our country clubs and on residential streets.

They have come into cities from a wide range of backgrounds. The roof rat comes from Europe, but may have originated in Asia. The pigeon is descended from the rock dove of southern Eurasia and North Africa. The various species of parrot arrived through the pet trade from Africa, South America, and Australia. The opossum, though it is a North American native, has immigrated from the South and the eastern areas of Texas. And the coyote, the two skunk species, and the crow are native Californians.

The upshot of this immigration is that Los Angeles has become a truly pluralistic society, with hundreds of animal and plant species living cheek by jowl in the human melting pot. However, like all new arrivals, animal immigrants need certain skills, traits, and abilities in order to compete with other creatures, take advantage of opportunity, and cope with human beings. They need what amounts to an angle.

Size plays a significant role. In Western society, there seems to be a definite size limit to wild animals, or even domestic animals, that we will permit to roam freely. (East Indian society is more liberal and will tolerate monkeys, peacocks, and cattle, but not elephants, loose in the streets.) The coyote is probably at the upper limits of acceptable size for America. Anything larger cannot hide, cannot function among us, without being harassed mercilessly. As uninvited guests, skunks, opossums, and rats benefit greatly from being able to fit into the cracks of society: in woodpiles and hedges, beneath rafters, inside walls—the list is endless.

Markings and coloration are also crucial. Roof rats, for instance, blend into the shadows with their plain, dusky browns and grays. So do opossums and coyotes. Skunks, on the other hand, benefit from advertising the fact that they are armed, displaying the most striking contrast of white on black.

Sound is the complement of visibility, and there seems to be a simple relationship between animal noise, agility, and alertness. In general, uninvited mammals are quiet mammals—the slower and less alert, the quieter. The slowest and dullest is the opossum, and it is virtually voiceless; rats, while quick, alert, and fast, squeak only during stressful encounters; even coyotes, which run extremely fast and are exceedingly alert, remain silent in the city.

Birds, however, are exempted from this rule. Parrots and crows squawk and screech like common rock music: they have the ultimate agility of flight and enjoy the privilege of being noisy.

Most urban wildlife are characterized by general habits and catholic tastes. A generalist is adaptable. In nature it lives in a range of environments. It is usually an omnivore, eating everything from vegetables, grass, and nuts, to freshly killed insects, birds, and mammals, to carrion of various stripe.

A specialist, on the other hand, survives naturally only in particular places. The ivory-billed woodpecker is a classic example. Before it became extinct it lived only in mature forests with their complement of dead trees and ate a strict diet of the beetle larvae that lived in the dead wood. When the forests were logged and the dead trees removed, the ivory-bill was exterminated.

In general, urban wildlife are opportunistic generalists. Not only can these animals live in various environments, but they also have the psychological flexibility to take advantage of new habitats. The common pigeon started out as a bird that nested in cliffs. Today it nests on highrise ledges, beneath rafters, under freeway overpasses, and in any other structure that suggests the ancestral environment. When the window of civilization opened, the pigeon flew right in.

As for intelligence, we like to think that any creature that persists uninvited among us has got to be bright. The truth is not so complimentary. Standard intelligence—the ability to learn and to solve problems—is clearly unnecessary. Insects have almost no intelligence at all, and the ubiquity of the cockroach demonstrates how much that matters. The pigeon, which is dull-witted compared to the crow, gets by in spectacular fashion. The opossum, perhaps as dim-witted as the pigeon, is among the most successful of wild urban creatures. Only the raccoon and the coyote would rank as intelligent urban beasts.

Of all the mental categories, temperament is probably the most important. Temperament is a cluster of emotional traits that lie beneath intelligence—traits such as nervousness, alertness, combativeness, shyness, robustness, persistence, tenacity, and so on. Temperament determines whether an animal can cope with the stress of an environment crawling with humans.

Stress can be alleviated to some extent through habituation. If raised around people, or with enough exposure later in life, almost any wild creature will grow accustomed to human company. But some individuals—indeed, some species—never seem to, at least not enough to live among us. They have the wrong temperament.

On the other hand, even though temperament is essentially genetic it is a direct expression of the genetic constitution—and cannot be fundamentally changed by nurture and habituation during an individual's life, it can be changed over a series of generations through genetic selection. An individual with a different temperament can be crafted by selective breeding. This can be accomplished artificially, as it is, for example, among dog breeders, who have created breeds as high-strung, snappish, and yappy as the chihuahua, as low-key, phlegmatic, and taciturn as the basset hound, and as psychotic, neurotic, and paranoiac as the American pit bull terrier. Even within litters there is often a remarkable range of temperaments, and each distinctive individual can be used through selective breeding to create a line expressing the traits peculiar to the founder.

Urban wildlife, then, almost certainly testifies to the emergence of new temperaments, animals who can tolerate the noises, the dangers, the crowded and restricted conditions of the city. Those who have been able to endure the city environment have passed their abilities on to their offspring, who are rewarded with access to the avocados.

The adjustments are tricky, though. Tolerance and familiarity must be counterbalanced with wariness and alertness; a wild animal cannot get too relaxed, too blasé. To retain its integrity it must retain in its genetic constitution its defiance, its wariness, and whatever gives it that psychological edge. This is why most wild animals do not become good pets, no matter how much training and love are lavished on them while growing up. If they appear stable and placid, it is an illusion. The wild temperament is always there, loaded and cocked.

Here, then, we have an overview of the gambits, traits, and abilities that wild creatures have utilized in their campaign to succeed in Los Angeles. Many have succeeded. Some have succeeded in phenomenal fashion. All have made it on their own terms, avoiding the genetic humiliation of domestication and retaining ownership of their souls.

Let us portray a few of the more gracious guests who now make their home in the city of avocados. In a bizarre, modern way, this city is the true avatar of Eden, with myriads of humans cohabiting with myriads of wild creatures.

OPOSSUM
(Didelphis virginiana)

Marsupial mammals are not native to Europe or Asia; indeed, Europeans were incredulous at the idea of raising one's young in a pouch of skin designed expressly for the purpose. The first marsupial ever seen by European eyes, a female opossum from South America, created a sensation in the year 1500, when it was presented to King Ferdinand and Queen Isabella of Spain. They could not contain their astonishment; both monarchs "placed their hands into this pouch and marveled greatly thereat," according to eyewitness accounts—this despite the fact that the creature had been dead for nearly two months.

The opossum has become the most noticed of the mammalian guests in Los Angeles. Departments of animal control receive more calls on opossums than on any other wild creature, usually along the lines of· "There's a giant rat in my backyard. It has a long pointed face, a naked tail, and it's as big as a cat!"

The opossum's high profile proves beyond a doubt that intelligence is not necessary for dealing with humans; it is without question the least intelligent mammal in America, the only possible competitor being the armadillo. Its cranial capacity is about one-tenth that of a fox, a placental animal of equal size. Like all marsupials, the opossum's brain has small cerebral hemispheres with few convolutions, and the right and left sides are not connected as they are in placentals.

Learning, too, is severely curtailed. Captive opossums, for instance, do not even succeed in distinguishing their owners from other people. Nor do they learn to associate traffic with danger, which amounts to a kind of blindness. That and the creature's slow, delayed reactions are the main reasons so many opossums die on streets and highways. Yet still their numbers grow.

What, then, is the secret to the opossum's success? Diet is certainly key. Opossums thrive on garbage and backyard fruits, on snails and slugs and insects, on birds' eggs and lizards and snakes—on whatever is available. They are also suited to the city by their innate habits and likes. Opossums take instinctively to the seams of society. Creatures of the night, they are active when people are not; and they are quiet—for all practical purposes, they are voiceless. They climb well, because their naked tails are prehensile and their hind feet possess an opposable thumb for grasping and holding. Fences thus become a system for backyard transit, safe from dogs.

Even the opossum's nesting habits match the shape of the suburban ecosystem, for shelter beneath low shrubs, under woodpiles, in empty garages, and in other nooks and crannies that people tend to ignore.

As for defense, opossums have fifty teeth and strong jaws. They are capable of delivering a rousing bite. However, if attacked by a serious adversary like a dog or a human being, they feign death. It's an effective ploy. Insects, snakes, and a host of other animals use it.

Reproduction is another key to the opossum's success. Opossums are capable of breeding year-round, bearing perhaps two litters of four to ten babies each. The young are born as embryos, no larger than a bumblebee, after just twelve or thirteen days of gestation. They crawl into their mother's pouch, fasten to a teat, and remain there for about two months. After leaving the pouch, they often ride on the mother's back.

COYOTE
(Canis latrans)

The coyote and the opossum are both generalists and opportunists, but they go about their business at the polar ends of style. Whereas the opossum shuffles dimly and stolidly through its existence in the space of a few backyards, the coyote descends into the city from the chaparral cover of the foothills with its awareness glittering and its wit flashing. With its elastic stride, this shrewd, cunning, and wild cousin of the domestic dog can easily cover ten or fifteen miles in a night of normal rounds.

William Wirtz, a professor of biology at Pomona College, has given us some idea of just how opportunistic this omnivore is. In the late 1970s and early 1980s, Wirtz studied coyotes in Glendale and Claremont, two suburbs of Los Angeles. He found an interesting difference between the two groups. Garbage made up 78 percent of the diet for the Glendale coyotes, but accounted for only 2.5 percent of the diet in the Claremont group.

It turned out that in Claremont the city required all garbage cans to be equipped with spring-loaded lids that closed automatically and could not be jimmied by dogs or other animals. As a result, the Claremont coyotes had no choice but to hunt the wild prey and native produce in vacant lots and undeveloped land. They ate rabbits, wood rats, insects like grasshoppers, cats (only a few), birds, and domestic fruit. Most of these coyotes moved back and forth between the foothills and the urban setting.

As for the Glendale coyotes, although they also moved down from the hills each night, instead of hunting the vacant lots and public lands, they ran down the alleys and raided garbage cans, which were not self-closing and self-locking.

Wirtz learned other things as well. Over the course of his studies he fitted six coyotes with radio collars and kept track of them twenty-four hours a day. Five of them lived in the foothills and only came into the city to forage. But one of them, a female, lived her life within the Claremont city limits and raised a litter in a vacant lot.

Coyotes often pass for dogs, a stroke of fortune that cannot be overlooked. People tolerate coyotes out of love for dogs, and inevitably they take the next step and put out food. Here we have another of those peculiarly human dilemmas: You want to help another living thing; compassion wells up inside you. And yet to feed these wild creatures is ultimately to threaten their existence and, often, to take their lives.

Free food corrupts wildlife. Wild things grow dependent on handouts. They become lazy and lose their fear and wariness. But they are not tame animals; they are not domestic. Their genes have not been molded to fit the human mind. Inevitably some well-intentioned but ignorant human will try to pet one of these creatures, or pick it up, often from the self-serving assumption that the animal senses their good intentions. The animal lunges so fast the hand cannot pull back, so fast the mind cannot react; in a split-second of horror, the fangs sink into flesh, tear and wrench, and another wild animal is condemned to death as a danger to humanity.

In Southern California, this scenario occurs with coyotes and people twelve to fifteen times per year. (To keep things in perspective, consider the twenty-six thousand cases of dog bite per year in the same region.)

Everyone who studies the interaction of wildlife and people arrives at the same conclusion: wildlife (with the exception of songbirds) should not be fed. It is a matter of intellect controlling the more tender human urges; but it leads to a higher good. William Wirtz found that the city of Claremont attracted only a few coyotes on a regular basis, and these foraged for their traditional food. Glendale, however, attracted many coyotes, and these appeared to be subsidized on garbage. They had become bag animals.

THE SKUNK
(Mephitis mephitis & Spilogale putorius)

The skunk, like the opossum, is considered a dim-witted creature. The first time you encounter a wild one, your first thought is that it's tame: it goes about its business without paying you the slightest attention. This leads directly to a second impression: maybe it's deaf and is unaware of you. You might walk over for a closer look. Suddenly it swings its body around, pointing its rear in your direction.

Your third impression is that you have been tricked into range. Of *course* it noticed you. Your heart skips one or more beats. You know instinctively that the strange stance, with the tail raised, is ominous. And what about that little pink circle of flesh aimed directly at your face like a gun port?

Your intuitive dread is quite appropriate. The skunk possesses a piece of chemical ordnance that sprays accurately up to six feet and carries well over twelve feet. It delivers several rounds of a caustic, oily musk that reeks so badly it can cause a person to vomit. The odor adheres for days. The only remedy is the time-honored trick of bathing in tomato juice.

Therefore, the skunk's nonchalant behavior is the result not of stupidity, but of confidence. In light of its powers, its fearlessness makes perfect sense. So do the stark, black-and-white markings: They advertise the animal's foul weapon and (for the most part) fend off trouble before it happens.

Two species of skunk are found in Southern California. The striped skunk (*Mephitis mephitis*) is the larger, averaging around six pounds. It has black fur with a thin white stripe down the middle of its forehead; the broad stripes for which it is named begin at the nape, spread out into a V behind the shoulders, and proceed to the rump, with the tail usually ending in a white tip. The spotted skunk (*Spilogale putorius*) is much smaller, averaging less than two pounds. It, too, is black, but it has a white spot on its forehead, one under each ear, four broken stripes that meander along the neck and sides, and a white tip to its tail.

Both species take readily to civilization and gravitate to basements and the cool spaces beneath houses. The young have a bad habit of exploring the narrow spaces between walls, on occasion getting lost or trapped and dying there. If all goes well, though, the mother skunk and her kits will eventually sally forth into the neighborhood—usually at night, but sometimes during the day. It is then that their innate confidence can get them into trouble, for skunks are vulnerable to predators that cannot smell (hawks and owls), that have never encountered a skunk before (dogs or inexperienced wild predators), that carry disease (especially rabies), and that are desperately hungry (coyotes in particular).

They are also vulnerable to humans. A young man by the name of Jerry Dragoo captures skunks in pursuit of his doctorate in biology at Texas A&M University. Dragoo proceeds like this: he merely walks over and hoists the animal by its tail. He jokes that he has no friends, or that friends think of him when they see a dead skunk on the road. He claims that his landlord has threatened to evict him, and that no one wants to steal his truck. But he has an intimate knowledge of the skunk and what the creature is really like.

They can make good pets. Dragoo's most recent companion was

a skunk he calls Penny—or Mom, as a result of the eight kits she bore not long after she and Dragoo began cohabiting. One of Penny's more endearing traits was to climb onto Dragoo's lap when he ate graham crackers and take them from his mouth. She was such a docile creature that he never had her scent glands removed, and eventually he released her back to the wild, defenses intact.

Not all skunks are so constituted. They show a wide range of temperament. While some become almost as docile as pets within minutes of capture and never resort to chemical force, others never grow used to people. With them, one has merely to think about approaching their cage and they cut loose with a salvo of spunk.

When not living as pets with people, skunks do very well as uninvited guests. They are probably beneficial in the grand scheme of urban ecology because they eat worms and insects, especially beetle larvae and cutworms, and they capture mice whenever they can. On the other hand, they dig up lawns and gardens in search of these items, and also eat the underground parts of plants—bulbs, corms, and so on. They are winners, though, these little stinkers, for they refuse to leave the city, and no one has ever figured out how to make them go.

CROW
(Corvus brachyrhynchos)

Stop sometime when you're walking along and you come upon a crow. Watch it as it stalks about on a lawn or in the street, as it sits on a branch, well removed from harm's way. Fix your eyes on this brash black bird and simply stare. Very soon it will start to fidget, flap its wings, stand and squat, stand and squat, debating whether to jump into the air and fly farther away. Finally it *will* jump up and fly off, landing high in some nearby tree, and there it will sit, regarding you with suspicion.

Then, another time, try a different ploy. Stop a few feet away, but this time take great care not to look in its direction; bend down and tie your shoes, stop and read the paper, examine a daisy. Now this fine, big guest will hold its ground. It seems to know that the eye of man portends many things, very few of them good for crows.

There is no better example than the crow of the balance between alertness and indifference that an uninvited guest must strike. It must be alert, but it must also be comfortable; it cannot tolerate the emotional trauma of an unceasing fight-or-flight response. Its temperament must therefore be adjusted toward a certain tolerance of human presence. This can be partly achieved by growing up around humans, but it probably requires some genetic adjustment to counteract the effect of the creature's recent history.

Crows have been persecuted and slaughtered for decades in the United States. Bounties have been placed on their heads. An industry grew up around crow-hunting paraphernalia such as calls, blinds, camouflaged clothing. The result was a strong evolutionary selection for vigilance. Crows are innately wary and probably could not tolerate cities at that point.

Then, maybe thirty years ago, crows began to invade the suburbs of Southern California, where they found a niche in the abundant trees and shrubbery. Now they are as much a part of the neighborhoods as the people.

Crows thrive in urban environs primarily because they can fly. Shooting is illegal in most cities, which also protects the crow. But crows have also succeeded in cities for the usual dietary reasons: they eat almost anything and are opportunistic enough to take over a wide range of habitats. They nest high above the ground in trees like palms and eucalyptus. They are highly intelligent and extremely social. Tens or hundreds of alert eyes are almost impossible to dupe.

Carolee Caffrey, a doctoral candidate in biology at UCLA, has been studying crow behavior for five years. She calls them "guys" and spends hundreds of hours observing them as they go about their lives on the Balboa Golf Course, which they have claimed as their own—learning in the process how to interact with the golfers.

In order to tell her guys apart, Caffrey has to mark them, and to mark them she must capture them. Early on she discovered that trapping and handling her subjects made such a negative impression that they would never again let her get close enough to observe. Now when Caffrey traps crows, what you see is a young woman with blue spiked hair, an enormous wax nose, black-rimmed, thick-framed glasses, and a moustache. Whenever *that* woman shows her face on the golf course, the crows flee in cawing multitudes. However, when the unadorned Carolee Caffrey shows her real face on the course there is no reaction whatsoever, which is exactly what she wants.

What she has found is the equivalent of an avian soap opera. The crows have divided the course into territorial tracts, each family owning its own property. They coexist peacefully, more or less, but there are special friendships and squabbles, and crows leaving town and crows coming back. The "kids" act much like human kids: Some leave home a few months after learning to fly, while others stay around and hang out with their parents. Some of the young that remain at home stay on for a year or more and help to feed and rear the next generation. Others just stay and freeload. Still others leave early but come back the next year and, rejoining their parents, help to rear the family. It's as if they have their eyes on the future and hope to inherit the family estate. And that may in fact be what happens. The golf course tracts may be passed down, generation to generation.

PARROTS
(*Amazona finschi, A. viridigenalis, A. oratrix*)

Parrots are not uninvited guests. They were invited to Southern California in cages. (Parrots are among the few creatures that can be taken from the wild as chicks and made into pets.) Inevitably some escaped or were set free, and for seventy or eighty years they have been living among us on their own devices. With their shrieks and

cries they are among the few who can cut through the anthropocen-
tric trance in which average humans live their urban lives—and
amusing it is to see people standing on the sidewalk transfixed, peering up into the branches of a tree, admiring another species.

Parrots get free by chewing through the bars of inappropriate
cages; their beaks are designed to crush tropical seeds and nuts and
tear the husks off tropical fruits, and a bamboo cage is barely a good
day's work. Parrots routinely escape through windows and doors.
Some were set free in 1913 for exotic atmosphere on an estate in Pas-
adena. Several hundred were released by smugglers in the early
1950s when the law closed in during a parrot bust in Alhambra. Another group escaped in 1961 when the Bel Aire fire consumed private aviaries. And all along people have released the parrots, whose
wrenching shrieks and violent yawps they could no longer stand.
No wonder, then, that the commonest species in pet stores are also
the commonest species in the urban wilds of Southern California.
These include yellow-headed Amazons (*Amazona oratrix*), red-
crowned Amazons (*A. viridigenulis*), and lilac-crowned Amazons
(*A. finschi*), as well as canary-winged parakeets (*Brotogeris versi-
coloris*), black-hooded parakeets (*Nandayus nenday*), and rose-
ringed parakeets (*Psittacula krameri*).

Oddly enough, even though these big, strong flyers no longer
find themselves behind bars, they seem just as rigidly contained by
circumstance. They have never invaded the native, undeveloped
regions of California, but stay tied to the older urban areas, which
are lushly planted. It seems that parrots depend for a living on the
hundreds of exotic tree and shrub species that have been imported
for shade and ornamentation and happen to produce fruits.

Parrots, unlike so many of the other uninvited guests, are strict
herbivores. Yet within their herbivorous diet they are generalists,
for they take a wide range of fruits, seeds, and nuts. They love apricots, for instance—but eat only the pits, not the flesh. On the other
hand, they eat the flesh of Japanese persimmons, not the seeds. All

told, parrots feed on at least thirty-four varieties of exotic produce, including English walnuts, plums, liquidambar pods, camphor seeds, eucalyptus nuts, tulip tree seeds, pecans, cherry seeds, carob, juniper berries, and various blossoms (but, oddly enough, not bananas or oranges). In fact, most of the items they eat do not exist in their native lands, and they have had to acquire new tastes here. The only California item on their list is the seed pod of the Western sycamore.

As for the private lives of parrots, everything revolves around the pair bond. Parrots mate for life, and they are virtually inseparable. In some species the pair even complete each other's calls, in a behavior known as "antiphonal duetting": One begins the phrase, the other picks it up in midarc and finishes it. When close together and hidden by foliage, they sound like a single bird; when they are separated, they sound like a single stereophonic bird. The two feed together, sleep together, fly together, raise their chicks together. If you look closely at a flock in flight, you will see that it is actually an aggregation of pairs.

In their native land, parrots usually form flocks with others of their own species. Because the drive toward flock foraging is very strong, they tend to do the same here as well; however, since their numbers in Los Angeles are limited, they often make do with whomever they can attract and form melting-pot mixtures of multiple species. Hybrids do occur.

At night parrots roost in very tall trees with dense foliage. The canopy protects them from the wind and helps them retain body heat. A flock entering the roost for the evening is indeed an unforgettable sight. The shrieks and cries build to a deafening crescendo, with pairs jockeying for position, new arrivals trying to wedge themselves in, established residents being shoved out. Then a single bird will give a strange, piercing cry, and instantly the din stops, as if some avian maestro had waved his baton, cutting off the climax with absolute precision.

There is one great unknown regarding the parrots of the Los Angeles megalopolis. Have these exotic birds truly taken root? They breed and raise chicks, no doubt about it, but does the number they produce balance the death rate? We do not know. The continuous arrival of new escapees certainly adds significant numbers. In terms of breeding, even in their native state many parrots appear to have a low reproductive rate, and the same is true here. Parrots nest in cavities, the number of which is limited. Let us hope there are enough. Parrots add class to the Los Angeles population.

ALLIGATOR LIZARD
(Gerrhonotus multicarinatus)

Reptiles have done poorly in the city, even though food abounds: insects and small rodents thrive in urban settings. At one time, before the city grew, snakes and lizards also thrived. Obviously, something happened, and that something surely involves the loss of good habitat. Gone are the large expanses of tall grass, low shrubs, and unpaved river and streambeds on which reptiles rely for cover. They are completely vulnerable when caught in the open.

One reptile, however, has been able to surmount the inhospitality of tar and cement. It is called the alligator lizard.

The alligator lizard is not a cute creature. It has a long, flexible body and four minuscule legs that hardly serve to push the creature along. It sinuates when it moves, flicking its forked tongue in and out, and is able to grasp branches and twigs with its tail. All in all, it looks like a snake in a lizard suit. The name "alligator" probably comes from the creature's mode of defense, for when cornered it gapes malevolently, lunges, and bites.

Alligator lizards succeed in the suburbs because they live hidden lives. They spend most of their time in ivy beds, in lawns overgrown with foxtails, in woodpiles, under shrubs—in other words, in dense cover. These lizards also succeed because they are generally sluggish and inactive. They don't do much rustling about, attracting the astute ears of predatory mammals.

There are, however, two perils for the alligator lizard. One is hot weather. Prolonged heat drives them in search of deep shade and water, and in late summer and early fall they appear in swimming pools, houses, and bathtubs. The encounter can be traumatic for those who don't know what an alligator lizard is.

The second peril comes with the mating season. In the spring, alligator lizards grow restless and reckless in their search for mates. They leave their cover, fall victim to cats, and are brought home as a prize—much to the disgust of the cat's human, who is doubly revolted by the bloody stump of the tail. Like many lizards, the alligator lizard has a tail designed to separate easily from the body and then explode in a thrashing, whipping reflex of amputation. When a predator gets a grip on the tail, the tail is jettisoned; the reflexive frenzy then holds the predator's attention, and the lizard has a chance to escape.

Like almost all lizards, the alligator lizard is a benign creature. It does no harm, poses no danger; if anything, it is beneficial. It eats slugs, snails, and ground-dwelling bugs and larvae. It is the kind of guest who causes as little bother as possible.

ARGENTINE ANT
(*Iridomyrmex humilis*)

Of all the insects that thrive in the technological civilization of Southern California, the Argentine ant may be the most irritating, the most universally present, the most inescapable. To Argentine ants, nothing is sacred. Everyone seems to suffer their incursions, even in apartments several stories above the ground. At any time of day or night you may find them crawling across the living room rug, the bathroom ceiling, even from an electric outlet. You may wake up with ants in bed or come down in the morning to ants streaming across the kitchen floor. What could they possibly want in the filing cabinet, in a closet full of clothes? If you could make all buildings vanish, leaving just the ants behind, suspended in air, you would still have the outlines of civilization.

Why are these ants so ubiquitous?

The answer has to do with a few profound changes in the ants' social biology. In the classic society of ants, a colony has one queen, and this queen, and she alone, lays eggs. The colony is essentially a queen surrounded by her children, the workers, which are sterile females. The Argentine ant is polygynous: it has many queens in each colony, perhaps as many as eight queens per thousand workers, and this elevates the colony's reproductive power to stratospheric levels.

Argentine ants are also polydomous: One colony occupies many homes. Most ants have a central nest, where all activities are concentrated. The Argentine ant alters that basic pattern by spreading its colonies out during the spring and summer, making a network of smaller subcolonies among which the workers and queens freely pass. It is much like a human megalopolis, like Los Angeles itself.

These two alterations of ant biology—multiple queens and undetermined boundaries—make the Argentine ant the insect equivalent of a multinational corporation. It has overwhelming power.

For all practical purposes, the Argentine ant is invulnerable because there is no one queen whose death would kill the entire colony. Because workers can move about freely and contribute to a large number of nests, they do not waste time and effort fighting among their own kind; all expended energy adds directly to the welfare of the megalopolis. And this ant is oh, so efficient. The queens are highly mobile, sometimes running in the worker column; thus the subcolonies can travel like little panzer divisions, bivouacking wherever the resources lie, moving on when they run out. Normally they nest outside human habitation, but they will at times set up nests inside the walls of houses, and especially in the soil of potted plants.

In addition to its foraging strength, the species is a dominating competitor with other ants. It possesses a chemical weapon called iridomyrmecin that can kill or repel violently. Armed with its chemical arsenal and its astronomic fertility, the Argentine ant has forged a virtual monopoly on ant industry in California cities. An exotic species, native to South America, it arrived in New Orleans sometime before 1871, showed up in Ontario, California, in 1905, and wherever it has set up operations it has essentially eliminated the native species.

If this ant has a weakness—and it may well not—perhaps it is its diet. Like other uninvited guests, the Argentine ant is an omnivore; it will eat insects, earthworms, infant field mice, candy bars, and meat scraps. But all that is supplemental. For its staple diet it devours honeydew—the sweet, sugar-laden excrement of aphids, soft scales, mealybugs, whiteflies, leafhoppers, and related sap-sucking insects. Honeydew makes up more than 70 percent of the ant's food. For that reason, Argentine ants shepherd these sap-sucking providers, carrying them up plants and trees to plant them safely on leaves, driving off the predators and parasites that would otherwise keep their numbers down. As a result, the aphids, mealybugs, scales, and so on explode in number.

But there may lie the Achilles heel. If whole neighborhoods were to unite, it might be possible to block the ant from its energy source. People could circle the trees and bushes with wide bands of Tanglefoot or Vaseline; they could cut off branches that touch houses and other plants; and maybe, just maybe, they could keep the ants from thriving on their ambrosia. People, after all, must be opportunists too.

CELLAR SPIDER
(*Pholcus phalangioides*)

Wherever *Homo sapiens* settles, there settles the cellar spider. Cellar spiders pitch camp in attics, cellars, toolsheds, garages, and un-

kept hallways, where they hang upside down in their shapeless, cha-
otic webs. They are harmless spiders with long, threadlike legs and
look almost identical at first glance to daddy longlegs. Daddy longlegs, however, are not spiders at all, for their body is a compact,
oval unit. True spiders possess a bicameral body—an abdomen
joined by a narrow stalk to a thorax—which holds the legs. Like all
spiders, cellar spiders are predators, but they are general predators.
They will eat almost any kind of insect that blunders into their
webs. They wrap their victims in cerements of spider silk and, having sucked them dry, cut them loose so they drop to the ground and
accumulate in a small dump of pelletlike cadavers.

One of the special traits that suits the cellar spider to life among
Homo sapiens is, simply, its preference for human buildings, which
provide protection, warmth, and dryness. What more could a creature want? A related aspect is the spider's preference for practical,
rough-hewn quarters like its eponymous cellar, toolsheds, outdoor
hallways, garages, and the dark, secret corners and nooks that
people shun.

Yet another reason for the creature's success is its reproductive
rate. Unlike most spiders, cellar spiders are semisocial, and males
and females often live next to each other in a productive relationship of pure convenience. The females bind their eggs in a thin,
translucent sack, which they hold in their chelicerae ("jaws") until
the spiderlings hatch, wee creatures that quickly scurry to find their
own nook or cranny.

When threatened, the cellar spider spins hysterically. It hangs
upside down, holding on to its web with legs so thin that they merge
with the strands of silk. It then twists its body back and forth until it
becomes a blur, at the same time heaving itself up and down. The effect is a ghostly image that seems to disappear in the dingy light, an
impossible target. And if a spider gets dislodged, it falls to the
ground and runs away with that same wobbling, hysterical motion
It is in their genes, a trait for survival among people.

FERAL CAT
(*Felis sylvestris catus*)

Feral animals are domestic animals that reject dependence on humans and return to a life of self-sufficiency. Make no mistake, feral cats are wild creatures. Anyone who manages to corner one will attest to this fact.

Cats, in fact, are remarkable in this respect. Of all the domestic animals, only the cat seems to have kept enough of its wild nature to live in nature and yet still take on civilized behavior. Even when completely domesticized and docile, the cat reverts to its animal routine the moment it goes outdoors. Like all independent creatures, cats love and fight, patrol territories and participate in peck orders, hunt prey and ward off enemies. One moment a cat can be rolling in the dirt, clawing, slashing, biting, screaming, maiming its adversary; the next moment it walks through the pet door into its human's house, climbs onto a lap, and becomes a purring, cuddling pet, absorbing its benefactor's love. It is bicultural, a creature of two worlds.

Wild animals like the coyote can, for the most part, never be kept as pets. Even those few wild mammals, like the skunk, which can sometimes be tamed—even these require an owner who understands the trigger of wildness. But the cat can become either a completely wild beast or a wholly tame pet, purely by virtue of its treatment during childhood. If, between the ages of three and twelve weeks, it is handled and cuddled, it will, with the odd exception, become a pet; if it does not receive gentle human contact by six or seven weeks, it goes the way of the wild (although with a great deal of patience, love, and care, some feral cats do accept human care). This dual nature is stored in the genes; other cat species do not possess it. The range between these polar opposites is so vast that it seems almost metamorphic in the insectan sense, with one set of genes for the larva, another for the adult: two creatures in one lifetime.

This bicultural strategy is apparently quite successful. Cats have been sighted in the middle of the Australian outback, and they live in such wild and remote settings as uninhabited islands near Antarctica, where they have been taken by man, then abandoned. They also live in the ghettos of major cities, and in the mansions and palaces of Europe.

But it is the urban feral cats that are of interest here, for they have an intriguing sociology. Cities, with their range of socioeconomic classes among humans, likewise have a socioeconomic range of feral cats. Wherever the cat finds itself, it adapts. The life of the feral ranges from the dirtiest, most parasite-ridden and pitifully deprived subsistence to an almost idyllic combination of domestic and wild privilege.

At the bottom end of the scale, feral cats infest low-income neighborhoods. They lurk around docks, they skulk among the waterfront rocks, and from the dumpsters and garbage cans of the slums they glean a vile existence in which their gums grow diseased, their teeth rot, their hair becomes matted and greasy, and their bodies get infested with fleas, mites, worms, and a veterinary compendium of other diseases. Unlike omnivores such as opossums, coyotes, and skunks, cats are true predators; their digestive tracts are specialized for processing animal flesh. Even though they may eat french fries or stale pizza, they extract little nutriment from such alien garbage. They become run down, and run-down cats inevitably become diseased and verminous.

In addition to all their deprivations, they are forced by their overpopulated straits to fight continuously. These poor, depraved creatures live by the thousands in the degraded habitat of cities and continue to breed.

Their infections pass to the better parts of town. There a different breed of cat plays out the cards of life. A surprising number of feral cats live in middle-class neighborhoods, for the simple reason that they are able to pass as pets. The ironic fact is, many of the cats we see in our neighborhoods are not pets to anyone; they are freelance cats. They are as wild as the coyote that can pass for a dog. They have hit on the art of deception and raised it to sublime heights.

These cats stake out territories, urinating on prominent neighborhood and domestic landmarks as boundary markers; then they make their rounds, eating the food we put out for the rightful cat of the house. Should a cat door be available, fine, they will come right in and help themselves. That done, they will spray the couch, dining room table, or whatever impresses them as the most fitting obelisk to mark for addition to their empires.

Cats take up residence in parks, on college campuses, and on hospital grounds. Here they grow fat on the food that hundreds of people practically beg them to take. But in all cases, whether in neighborhoods or public grounds, you cannot get close enough to touch these cats.

How do these uptown ferals come to be? The obvious answer is that people abandon cats when they move. If you have to relocate and can't or don't want to take the cat, just leave it; some decent person will take it in. So rationalizes the departing neighbor. What often happens, though, is that the abandoned cat approaches a likely house and gets rejected. It might receive a good swift kick that injures its back, it might be hit with a heaved rock or doused with a hose on full bore. After a few of these chance encounters, the cat decides that direct introductions are not a good idea. Why not just take the food placed out for the resident cat?

Then the critical period of socialization comes into play. If the abandoned cat is a fertile female, she will bear her litter in some sheltered place beneath a bush or in the rundown woodshed out back. The kittens will be reared by the mother, with no human interaction during that critical period of receptivity; thus the domestic window of opportunity will close, creating a new group of feral cats. The young cats will look like pets, will participate in neighborhood affairs like domestic cats. But they will never assume the limp, purring postures of affection like their siblings raised in the company of people. Like the pigeon, the raccoon, the coyote, and other wild animals, the feral cat may habituate itself to the presence of people, but there it will draw the line.

That accounts for cats that become feral or stray (the terms are nearly interchangeable) through abandonment. But many cats decide on their own to pack up and leave. A survey done in the San Francisco Bay area found that about 60 percent of unaltered housecats become feral within three years. Why? According to the Feral Cat Working Party, an English organization that strives to better the lot of ownerless cats, there are twenty-three reasons in addition to the bombing of a city during all-out war. Let us content ourselves with three: competition with peers may drive cats away; indifferent or abusive humans can send them off; and, in the case of young, virile males, they may follow an irresistible urge to go out into the world and seek their own territory. Whatever the reason, the creature we think of as the domestic cat is actually a strategic genius that has its cake and eats it too.

And so it is that a considerable number of species have come to share our civilization with us. They have come into our space, looked about, and decided to stay. However, because they have not asked permission, which is to say they have rejected domestication and succeeded in society on their own terms, we view them as uninvited guests—and that is euphemistic. "Vermin" (with loathing) and "Wild animal!" (with horror) more honestly express the feelings that many humans harbor toward them.

But these creatures have merely retained their autonomy in the face of the most domineering and dictatorial species in the entire history of evolution, and for that they must be viewed with respect.

They have had to pay a price. They have had to exploit the seams where the niches lay, have had to inhabit the parking lots and gutters and cracks in the walls and attics and the weeds out behind the garage. If blessed with flight, some have been able to revel in prouder surroundings, but in most cases it is the places deemed worthless or, at best, unworthy of human attention that the animals have seized. Or they have occupied the night, the time that society concedes.

The price of autonomy is therefore integrity. Autonomy has been salvaged, but, in the course of salvation, has been corroded. For the squalid recesses of asphalt and concrete, drywall and stucco, gravel and sand, the uninvited guest has abandoned the vaulting dignity of ancestral places. They have had a choice; they could have remained in what is left of the wild. But the garden, laden with fruit, was irresistible, the choice inevitable. The avocado?—it is the apple of New Eden.

COCKROACH

|——————————————————————————————————||

MEMOIRS

I became an entomologist because of a conversation.

"Professor Stern, sir, could I ask you to write me a letter of recommendation to graduate school?"

"Oh, I think that could be arranged. Where do you want to go?"

"Let's see—Cornell, Minnesota, Duke, North Carolina State, San Diego State. I think that's it."

"What are you going to study?"

"Ornithology."

"Ornithology? What's wrong with insects? Why don't you go to Berkeley and study entomology?"

"Well, I'm not that interested in insects. I've always loved birds. Besides, my grades aren't good enough. I'd never get into Berkeley."

"Well, I got my Ph.D. there in entomology, and my major professor then is the chairman of the department now."

"Hmmmm. . . . Well . . . you know, insects really *are* interesting . . . and the more I think about it . . . the more interesting they become. I'd *love* to go to Berkeley and study insects!"

I had taken Professor Stern's course in the ecology of insects at the end of my junior year, and it had salvaged my college career. I was on academic probation at the time, subject to dismissal, and knowing that my future was rotating over the pit of failure I had finally applied myself to my studies, in part because of a good teacher.

Stern was the sort of professor a college boy could admire in the early 1960s. He was a big, square-faced, clean-cut man who wore plastic-rimmed glasses and white short-sleeved shirts with ties. As a young man he had ridden the rails from the Midwest, erupted from a boxcar somewhere in the great Central Valley of California, and landed running; he hadn't stopped until the war was over and the GI Bill had seen him through to the university post he now held. He was blunt, decent, good-hearted, with no affectations and no time for people who played games.

Stern was also an earnest, concerned teacher who asked creative questions, questions that required a student to think, not merely to memorize. The upshot was that Professor Stern reached me. I received an A in the course, and when the time came to plan my graduate school admissions campaign, Doc Stern was the man on whom I piled a heavy load of hope.

I was turned down by all my choices except San Diego State University, which was required by policy to accept me (and it did so with the proviso that I maintain a 2.5 grade point average), and the University of California, Berkeley. So off I went to the educational Camelot by the Bay of San Francisco in the fall of 1966, everything I would need to pitch camp piled into my red VW, my beetle. I found an apartment on Regent Street near Dwight Way, the ground floor of a white clapboard house no more than a hundred feet from what would become People's Park within the year, and I settled down to study insects. At least, that's what I thought I'd study.

Straightaway I had what proved to be a premonitory experience. One morning I sat down to breakfast, intending to read the *San Francisco Chronicle*, which I had brought in from the front porch. I slipped off the rubber band, and just as I opened to the front page this *thing* the size of a teabag exploded from the classified ads, flew flipping and scrambling through the air over to a pile of old papers by the fridge, and disappeared. As my feet left the floor and the *Chronicle* flopped toward the ceiling, I recognized the object for what it was— a specimen of the American cockroach, *Periplaneta americana.*

Grabbing an empty jar, I closed cautiously on the spot where the roach had disappeared, the Arts section, and gently, very, very gently, began opening the pages. The thing seemed to anticipate my moves, though, and before I could react it catapulted into the Metro section. I reached for that, and at the instant my finger touched paper it sprinted over the edge of the pile and wedged itself into the Classified Ads, Personal Message section. I pressed the paper down beyond the creature so it couldn't squirm away between the sheets, then lowered the jar.

Finding all escapes blocked, the roach then did what any creature would do in a similar predicament: it panicked. It scrambled hysterically, legs blurring, body bouncing off the sides of the jar, falling on its back, flailing onto its feet, and, finally exhausted, coming to rest with its head pressed to the floor.

It lay there looking forlorn—but not *being* forlorn, of course. Forlornity is a kind of self-pity, and self-pity requires self-conscious intellect; yet somehow this insect gave the impression that it did realize its predicament, that it did address the situation with something more than pure instinct. Then the tips of its antennae began to move, almost imperceptibly. Like tiny, thread-thin snakes they pushed into the juncture of glass and paper, the tips probing and poking, the shaft following flexibly behind, sliding next to the inside lip of the jar, caressing a crescent of paper with a personal message printed on it: "W. J.—It's formaldehyde disinfectant in water. —Louise." What becomes of one's words when they leave home and go out into the published world, my friend, is random fate.

I kneeled down to contemplate the prisoner. It lifted its head slowly, its antennae palpating the air in slow, alternating strokes, and gazed at me. Its eyes glinted in the morning sunlight. I knew that what looked like two huge eyes covering the contour of half the head were actually two honeycomb aggregations of ten thousand?—twenty thousand?—I didn't count—hexagonal lenses called ommatidia. Each ommatidium was said to form one point of light of a composed image in the creature's mind. The eyes looking back at me were supposed to create coarse pictures of reality, like very poor newspaper reproductions, or so the theory went. But what else lay behind the eyes? I knew this creature could have no intelligence. A soul? . . . absolutely not. These questions fascinated me. What laws, what programs, lay behind the actions of this small creature? What programs and laws informed my own brain? I had come here to study insects, but I knew then, somehow, face to face with a cockroach imprisoned in a jar atop the *Chronicle*, that the questions glinting from those strange, wonderful eyes would not end there. I knew that they would lead back someday to me and my own species.

Meanwhile, my academic rebirth got off to a rousing start. Realizing that the next step in my education would occur in Vietnam if I failed to pass muster at the University of California, I earned straight A's for the first year and a half of my graduate career. I was bearing down on the exalted title of Ph.D., doctor of philosophy, doctor of *insect* philosophy, and doing so well that I was asked to teach the laboratory of a course called Insect Morphology and Physiology, Entomology 102. Ah yes, and because the cockroach in its various species is the entomologist's answer to the laboratory rat, part of my duties would be to raise them in large masses. Purveyor of roaches, that was me.

The breeding and rearing were carried out in special containers called "cultures," originally intended to be garbage canisters. But they were light in weight, waterproof, and had tight-fitting lids into which windows could be cut for ventilation. On the container floor we placed four or five pieces of cardboard for shelter and tossed in a few handfuls of dried dog food. For the water supply we filled a small bottle and plugged it with a cotton wad. The roaches could chew on this to extract the moisture, but the fluid could not flow out and flood the colony. And to ensure that the roaches would not escape through the tiniest space between the container lid and lip (though inevitably some always did), we slathered Vaseline around the can's inside rim.

Depending on the needs of the course, I kept between five and eight cultures lined up in two rows down the middle of the roach room. These contained four species that more or less represented the world. I had barrels of German roaches (*Blattella germanica*), small, delicate creatures that scurried away like windblown feathers whenever they escaped; Madera roaches (*Leucophaea madera*), a beautiful gray species from Africa with what appeared to be veined leaves for wings; and Cuban burrowing roaches (*Byrsotria fumiguta*), two-inch wonders that gave off a sweet, fruity aroma and had bands of armor across their backs like living trilobites. And of course I reared the mainstay of the laboratory, the good old American roach (*Periplaneta americana*), the big brown water bug that scrambles behind the toilet or into the pantry when the lights come on. In the cockroach cultures, however, a scared roach had nowhere to go but under the cardboard, and if ever I lifted off a lid without warning, the garbage can would emit an explosive WHOOSH as several thousand roaches, German, African, Cuban, and American, dived hysterically for cover.

This universal reaction was just short of a seizure in its intensity, a panic in which a roach would hurtle, wings flapping and legs flailing, over anything in its way, including a human being. More than once, when I reached into a culture to grab a few roaches for some experiment, four or five individuals would scramble instantaneously up my arm, spring off into the room, and escape before I could so much as flinch. There's no denying it—the handling and rearing of roaches will never be called a pleasant task, but it *was* my job, and the job had an unannounced benefit: It started to reveal things about the people in the lab. I recollect one incident in particular. Shortly after I assumed command of roach production, I decided to stop on my way home one night and check the cultures. It was late, around 11:30, so I was surprised to find the lights on in the rearing room. I opened the door and found Arnold there. Arnold had taught the laboratory and tended to the needs of the roaches during the previous four years. He had taken me under his wing, as the saying goes, and tutored me in the art of cockroach care and maintenance.

Arnold, whom we had called "the Viking," blond and fair, ice-eyed, frozen-faced, monolith-minded, six foot four and massive. Arnold, who, when I had taken his course, had stood in the back of the room with arms crossed over his massive chest and scowled as we dissected our roaches and ran our tests. Arnold, with his eyes glaring back in the deep-set caverns of his skull. That same ironic Arnold whose hulking form completely belied his spirit. For Arnold was almost effeminate in his habits and sensibilities.

He cut his food in squares and aligned them corner-to-corner on the prongs of his fork. He carried Kleenex individually folded in perfect little squares. He fussed and dusted and washed compulsively to keep the lab and rearing rooms immaculate—the cleanest, most hygienic roach hotels the world has yet seen.

As I entered the room, Arnold was leaning over one of the culture cans. He appeared to be hugging himself, and I saw that he was clutching the canister lid in a kind of fetal embrace. I sensed that he was angry but had no way of knowing the extent of it.

"Hi, Arnold," I said, starting off with the gambit of cheerful nonchalance.

He ignored me, refused to turn around. For an instant I thought he was trembling.

"Arnold," I said, "is anything wro . . ."

Without the slightest warning, he whirled around. "GOD DAMN YOU," he bellowed in a dead, sepulchral voice that still reverberates from the walls of my memory. He picked up the entire roach container and thrust it at me.

"LOOK!"

I took the container and peered cautiously into it. There, at the bottom of the pit, was the worst sight I ever saw in Berkeley. One of the water containers had come unplugged, flooding the floor and turning the contents of the canister into a soup of dogfood and dissolved cardboard. A layer of dead roaches, mostly immatures, floated on top in a vile ferment of death.

I was deeply chagrined. Obviously I had not plugged the cotton wicks into the water bottles tightly enough; no one was to blame but me. I had eliminated from the face of the earth a thousand innocent roaches—and I do not say that lightly. All I could do was look up at Arnold's formidable countenance and beg forgiveness. But to my surprise I saw that his eyes were red and swollen. For a second or two I didn't understand; it was too incongruous. Finally it struck me that he was fighting back tears. The intensity of the moment was too much, however, and his grief burst loose with a great wrenching sob.

"The little ones," he bawled. "The eggs . . . they never had a chance!" And he lumbered from the room, moaning.

I was dumbfounded. Never, in the weirdest tales of entomology, had anyone been known to be devastated by the mass extermination of roaches. I realized, standing there with thousands of terrified roaches scrambling inside the various other cultures, that I and everybody else in the lab had taken Arnold at the value of his face and his monolithic mass. I saw now that Arnold's personality had been assembled without a sense of humor, without the ability to dance, soul to soul, with another person. He scowled and glowered because, try as he might, he could not communicate with humans, could not connect his kindness and love and deep loyalties with his own kind. If his own species could not or would not recognize his worth, he could only bequeath his kindness to the roaches. It seemed immensely sad, even pathetic, to see such goodness caged in a giant's soul, and I stood there and counted my blessings.

I settled into the daily routines. The tasks of freshening the water, providing kibbles, and changing the cardboard became rote. Inevitably, however, I would find myself watching the roaches as I went about my work. I began noticing the way they moved, the places they chose to rest, the push and shove of their personal interactions. It dawned on me one night that more was going on in the containers than met the casual eye. The roaches were going about their lives in a way curiously similar to the way we humans do. I began to wonder if Arnold might not have been so strange after all. I also began to find in the roaches a source of humor. But above all else, I caught my first glimpse of the kinship that unites the working of all brains, human, animal, or arthropod.

This kinship between roaches and humans first revealed itself in the area of aggression. One night I was feeding a colony of Madera roaches that had been without food for more than a week and were lying still, as roaches do, to conserve energy. I scattered a handful of dogfood across the container floor. Immediately a thicket of antennae began to wave, slowly at first, then faster and faster, as if the antennae were broadcasting excitement from roach to roach, brain to brain. As the intensity rose they began sprinting about in fits and starts, running a few inches, then stopping to palpate the air.

A young male missing half an antenna found the first nugget of food, a piece nearly as large as himself. He seized it in his mandibles and, to my utter surprise, dragged it over to a protected space between two slabs of cardboard. The way he behaved—alertly keeping his body between the prize and his peers, standing over the food while gnawing with an almost desperate urgency—was exactly the way a stray dog would work on a bone, or a child guard her teddy against a sibling. While I watched, another roach ran off with loot, then another, and another, until all the adults were standing over their food, protecting it while they ate. You could almost hear them growl.

I then witnessed something else, and the silent growls became invisible screams. I had seen evidence of sinister happenings without thinking much of it, since so many of the adults carried the stumps of amputated feet, legs, and antennae; it seemed almost normal in the cockroach cultures, a spurious artifact, perhaps, of crowded living. One night, though, the significance of these injuries became clear.

I was about to go home for the evening and thought I'd take a peek at the rearing room before I left. I glanced absentmindedly into the Madera barrel as I made a quick round of the room. My eye was drawn instantly to the tension of an incipient fight. Such tension is universal, whether acted out by insect or human, and the attraction is likewise riveting. Two males had squared off.

The opponents stepped deliberately closer, stopping about a half-inch apart. Slowly they crossed antennae and began feeling each other out. In a strange, ritualized ceremony, both extended their legs until they looked like little raised platforms. They stood there for a moment, then, as if a bell had rung, lunged into combat, grappling, biting, and rolling about on the floor. This went on for fifteen or twenty seconds until one of the roaches abruptly broke free and tried to escape. The victor, however, followed in close pursuit; the two skittered under the cardboard, dodged among the kibbles, and clambered up and down the container walls until, exhausted, they stopped to rest. The battle continued in several bouts separated by short rests, but eventually both roaches appeared to lose interest, and the conflict died out.

Although I never found out how this particular rivalry ended (I was never able to identify them again in the seething canister), the pair probably fought several times more. It turns out that cockroaches held in close quarters form peck orders much like domestic fowl, wolves, apes, and the higher social animals in general. A series of confrontations determines who's boss, whereupon the loser defers to the victor and usually backs off without further fighting.

During these cockroach struggles, victory was not always enough, and the winner chased his rival relentlessly, as if to humiliate him. In these cases the loser groveled. He lay down, tucked his legs under his body, folded his antennae back along his sides, and tried to endure while the dominator chewed on his legs, wings, antennae, even on the edges of his dorsal plates, inflicting the damage I had noticed earlier.

On rare occasions, the loser died of stress. That, at least, is what we presume; it has been observed by other students of the cockroach, and no one has put forth a more plausible explanation. There were no wounds, no signs of damage. Thoroughly defeated, the male would lie down and simply remain there until, at some imperceptible point, his life slipped off to eternity and rigor mortis seeped in.

It was disturbing, somehow, that a young, vigorous creature, his entire life ahead, would give up in passive suicide. Even to a roach's brain, the prospect of interminable subordination and domination was evidently not worth the living. The next day I would find an entomological specimen. In the case of death by stress, the victim would become an exquisite shell of life, with the antennae, wings, legs, claws, and hairs still in perfect order.

Up to this point, about three years into my career as purveyor of roaches, I had assumed that such incidents were amusing parallels to human behavior and nothing more. To think that there might be some commonality in the workings of the animal and the human mind was ridiculed by the university crowd, who called it by the grandiloquent term "anthropomorphism." The term meant blasphemy: Read not the motives of Man into the dim-witted brains of vermin. The very premise was also, of course, arrogant and self-aggrandizing, a kind of humanistic P.R. job. One cannot use the term "anthropomorphism" without presuming a grand rift, a kind of holy chasm between the minds of animal and man that can never be bridged. Humans march to the tune of the rational mind, while abysmal creatures like the cockroach follow blind urges and deaf desires called instincts.

Yet I couldn't dismiss what I had seen. In some nagging way the notion of anthropomorphism went against biology. What if the intellectual establishment had it backward? What if, instead of imputing human thought to the animal mind, we should impute animal workings to the human mind? If indeed we had evolved from animals, what was the human mind but an extension of the animal's urges? But I was not yet ready to frame this idea, so I kept on observing.

Sexual relationships were another of life's issues on which the roaches had comment to make, because they emphasized the intimate relationship between courtship and sex on the one hand and aggression on the other. Like most creatures, cockroaches do not indulge in free sex; in fact, they're very choosy about their mates. Getting up a romance involves the twofold task for the male of shutting the female's defenses off and turning her desire on. In humans this can take hours, even days or weeks, but in roaches it usually takes minutes.

The Madera roaches had the most obvious moves. I soon noticed that the females didn't like to be approached by undesirable males, or even by desirable males at undesirable times, and violently rejected their advances. The female controlled the situation. When she felt desire, she released a pheromone, a scent that appeals only to members of the same species. The males wasted no time in responding. Their antennae waved slowly as the molecules of scent activated sensors along the shaft; the neurons leading from the sensors to the brain began to click with bioelectric pulses; and the pulsating neurons stimulated other neurons pressed side by side in a

larger cable of sensory nerves. After several moments of rising ex-
citation, the males would begin to dart about, first in one direction,
then, after stopping to test the air, in another. Eventually their random dashes brought them together with a female who was ready to
negotiate.

Contact made, a pair stood face to face, caressing and intertwin-
ing their antennae. The male, apparently realizing that the female's
interests were indeed prurient, then pivoted so the tip of his abdomen was almost touching her face. He fluttered his wings to blow his
own scent over her antennae and turned back around to see whether
it was having any effect. If so, the female would now be flapping her
wings impatiently. In a flurry of flailing antennae the male mounted
her like a tiny, tiny dog. There they rested for some time, completely
motionless except for the slowly waving antennae. The proceedings
evidently a "go," he then pushed himself off to the left, and still
tethered by his aedeagus, rotated around so that they stood, still
connected, facing in opposite but apparently compatible directions.

From this point on, a cockroach liaison was basically like a human relationship, at least so far as I could tell by watching. The pair
would stand around, for hours on end, absorbed in the introspective
task of transferring and storing sperm (for which the female has a
special sac known as the spermatheca). As long as there was no need
to move actively, everything was tranquil and relaxed. But sooner or
later something would happen, the worst case being the approach of
a human being, and an urgency greater than sexual bliss pre-empted
the pleasures of love.

Each member would attempt to bolt—in opposite directions.
Something would have to give. Seldom was it the relationship.
Roaches are sincere in their commitments, and once they join, they
are usually yoked together in a bondage of interlocking gonads until
the transfer of sperm is complete. No, what gave was the male.
Being smaller and lighter, he was dragged along backwards by the fe-

male, wings fluttering, legs clutching at kibbles, pieces of cardboard, other roaches, and writing in general frustration, while his bigger and stronger mate decided where the relationship was heading.

As time went on, incidents like these collected in my mind, a compendium of the cockroach condition. Taken alone, they were little more than amusing observations, but eventually experience and theory met, and the human implications of cockroach behavior came into focus.

I don't recall how it began, but I do remember realizing one day that, try as one might, it was almost impossible to sneak up on my roaches and not find them alert, even after they'd been left alone for hours. There they'd be, stroking the air with those ironically delicate, refined antennae, divining the news from molecules of air with Stradivarian refinement. It was impossible to suppress the feeling that they were, in some fundamental way, intelligent.

And the feeling was completely wrong—from the conventional, human point of view. The roach, measured for intelligence quotient, has almost none at all. Its mind is beneath stupidity; to be stupid one needs intellect, and the roach has nothing but instinct. It is strictly a monument to hard wiring. The cockroach has been shown to be capable of learning only the most rudimentary responses, like raising its legs to avoid a shock. In the interests of science, the creature is fastened in place, given an experimental cue, followed closely by a walloping shock. To make the science even more interesting, the roach is then decapitated and the headless corpse tickled with the pre-shock cue. The result is not merely interesting; it is fascinating. The legs pull up to avoid the shock, *without any advice from the brain*. The learning is in the peripheral nerves themselves!

Yet it was overwhelming to realize all that the roach could accomplish with its lowly instincts. One night, on the way home from the lab, I noticed a big female American roach walking in the street with a peculiar stiff-legged gait, like a child on stilts. I then noticed the remains of a peanut-butter-and-jelly sandwich, on which a stream of ants was converging. The roach had wandered into the crawling, stinging, biting multitudes, and she was reacting with the simplest and most effective of all defenses: holding her body above the masses and the flow. Intelligent? No. Learned? No. Just one of the instinctive programs wired into the roach's pinhead of a brain, programs that function remarkably like reason.

It struck me, looking down from my lofty altitude on this insect, that in the big view of things, all brains are intelligent. No, it sweeps wider still. *Biology* is intelligent. If you define the *fundamental* intelligence as the appropriate response to one's environment, then plants are intelligent; so are bacteria, fungi, even viruses.

Consider the intelligence of plants as they dance to the beat of the seasons. As winter wears on, plants mark the cold, and when they tally a certain time below a certain temperature, their physiology readies itself for the coming of warmth. With the onset of spring, plants measure the daylight and whether the day lengths are increasing or decreasing. Their physiology is crafted to act appropriately when the day reaches a certain length. Plants know in the mind of their physiology when preparations must begin again for winter: when the leaves must stop producing food, when the pigments of fall must be prepared, when the joints between stem and twig must be dissolved so the leaves can fall to the ground. The dance of life with earth is sublimely appropriate. Existence is intelligence.

What I watched, then, standing over the roach, under the glow of the streetlamps, was physiologic reason. On the level of blind, neuromechanical operation, reason and abstract comprehension are both built into the nervous system as fundamental properties. This idea, however, has to be read in the light of evolution.

Evolution is a cornerstone of modern biology. A student or professional academic cannot get through a day without nodding to this or that ramification of evolution theory, and eventually one becomes so familiar with the concepts and principles that they assume a style. There is a certain feel to the way evolution works, a stylistic imprint. Natural selection, the mechanism by which evolution works, spins in certain patterns, flows in certain courseways.

With me the process has gone beyond style. The day came when evolution became a full-blown character, whose looks and habits reflect the way he works. He is, to be blunt, a slovenly fellow. He does only what must be done to keep a species going, and he never attends to anything until the last minute. In my mind's eye he looks grubby, like a mechanic, or like Vulcan, the Roman god of blacksmithery. But he has the incongruous talent of a celestial jeweler. He works with molecules. His masterpiece is the miraculous necklace of DNA, and by working the molecular beads he creates dinosaurs, plants, bacteria the countless millions of species that have played their roles on earth since life began. We, with our enormously expanded brains, are merely another of those species.

One of Evolution's most intriguing operations is described by what might be called the Law of Used Parts. Everything Evolution makes, he makes from used materials. To make a lizard, he had to use the frog; to make a bird, he started with the lizard. The bird was tricky, a much harder job than making the lizard from the frog. The reptilian skeleton, the metabolism, the circulatory system, all had to be retooled. Evolution converted the front legs into wings, transformed scales into feathers, made the bones light and strong and hollow, connected the hollow spaces directly with the lungs for internal cooling in flight, and upgraded the eyes and nervous system for the split-second demands of aerial acrobatics. That is how Evolution always works: bending this, compressing that, lengthening, expanding, inflating, dividing, engraving, sanding, polishing.

So how did Evolution alter the monkey to create this mind of ours? There are, unfortunately, no witnesses. One thing, though, is clear. The human brain is a jury-rigged device, and the mind reflects that fact. A thin layer called the cerebral cortex generates conscious thought, they say, the kind of thought we label "reason." Evolution has laid the cortex over a region of gray matter three inches thick, a region that generates feelings, urges, intuitions, and desires. Reason is therefore wrapped around emotion—not, it seems to me, the best design for a machine whose purpose is to produce logic. Logic and the conscious mind are therefore driven by emotion. What chance does a thin membrane of reason have of containing a thick lump of urge and desire, impulse and reaction?

Why, the whole mechanism of conscious comprehension is an emotional thing! If you stop and turn your senses inward, you can even feel the mechanism work, can feel it churning about in that cluster of subconscious neurons called the reptilian complex, where the ancestral lizard still holds court, raising its crest toward rivals and prospective mates, scanning the world for enemies. The impulses that issue from the lizard's court pass on to the surrounding neurons, which form a center known as the limbic system or neopallium. It is the heirloom of the ancient mammal, that rodentine insectivore which emerged from the reptiles. The limbic system adds the feelings that produce the "four Fs"—fighting, fleeing, feeding, copulating—and this melange of ancestral urges comes roiling into the cerebral cortex, the brain's most recent layer, the layer of "reason." There it becomes a conscious thought as it is packaged into words, sorted into phrases and sentences, weighed and analyzed, and if deemed appropriate, emitted into the world through the mouth, the written word, the vote, the unspoken consent, or some other avenue of dispensation.

The process works both ways, of course, and conscious thoughts received from without are relayed down to the ancestral centers, which leads to dialogue with the world.

And what of humanity, that great summation of the entire species' thoughts and actions? Having to start with the monkey, how did evolution manage to fabricate the human's image of itself? A few modest speculations suggest themselves.

Take courage, for instance. A quality arising, perhaps, from the urge to resist domination by the very large male, the neighboring clan, the predatory beast. Evolution has a way of building character from such primitive parts. And genius—what primal traits has Evolution fused to produce that? Creative cleverness, without question, but just as crucial are the dashes of aggressiveness, persistence, and irreverence to produce boldness of thought, to defy convention and push beyond the boundaries of accepted and acceptable thought. Religious faith? Awareness must be at the core, an awareness chained by intelligence to that most primal of all urges, the urge to survive.

But a quick look around confirms the most primal of all anxieties: everyone dies; I isn't always going to be—oblivion. It is *almost* conceivable and the hairs rise. And the intelligent mammal runs back to the source of life, to the parent who brought its inchoate being into the world, nurtured, sheltered, and defended it, and, now grown into the adult stage, the intelligent mind conjures the adult parent, the omniscient, omnipotent, invincible concept that defends the soul. Infinity, eternity, cosmos: the anxieties of intelligent survival are all taken into account by the religious urge.

In the end the roaches revealed to me an overarching view of life which placed the human mind in a different perspective from the one mainstream society teaches its members. It is an eccentric vision without question. But it seems to conjure a sense of tolerance and comfort, for it recognizes the kinship of mind.

The insect brain is laid out in fundamentally different patterns than the brain of mammals, yet it generates behavior that is remarkably similar in dealing with the basic tasks of life. At least to that extent there seems to be a similarity of mind. The mammals, however, share the basic structures of brain, and the differences are a matter of degree. So is the mind; an honest person cannot avoid this conclusion.

In other words, the human mind is an extension of the animal mind—a variation on a theme—not a celestial novelty. Which means that intellect is essentially a weapon/tool wielded by the ancient appetites, anxieties, revulsions, moods, and kindred urges.

As my simple insects acted out their lives, I was struck by the intelligence of instinct, the appropriateness and common sense of actions designed for life in a certain place. I came to the conclusion that what we humans call common sense may, at its very foundation, be nothing more than good instincts. What we call the conscious mind might simply be a program that overlays the instincts, the innate intelligence of the unconscious nerves, and watches them operate. It is as if self-consciousness is the ability to monitor our programs (instincts?) and, at the right time, make connections among them, among memories, mechanical comprehension, emotions, urges. Maybe that is what we experience as rational thought.

The simple truth is, humans, like all animals, spend the majority of their lives pursuing food, territory, social position, and mates. The chase isn't quite as direct as it is with the less cerebral creatures; money complicates things. But money is nothing more than a tool for conducting the eternal quests.

Odd as such conclusions may seem, they didn't disturb me a bit. They were humbling, because they were universal. They included all living things. Morally neutral, they made sense of human excesses, of actions that a truly rational creature would never perform. In the end, I was amazed at what Evolution had made by exaggerating the monkey.

I do not want my cockroach memoirs to leave the impression that Evolution has no warts, for in truth there are some rather embarrassing flaws in its character. The evidence is shot like excess fat throughout the substance and essence of nature, and, consequently, throughout human nature as well.

Evolution is first and foremost a cheapskate. I did not want to emphasize this earlier, when I mentioned that it uses nothing but second-hand parts; that new species are always created out of old; that nothing is ever conjured, full blown, from new materials; but cheapness is what it comes down to, and inevitably it shows in the product. I shall illustrate this as soon as I dispense with the second flaw, that Evolution is, to be blunt, a confirmed sloven.

It deals with problems only when forced to. An ice age comes, and *then* it fashions fur coats, wasting countless lives in the process of natural selection. It never plans ahead, never prepares a species before the change occurs, but patches and sews and tries to keep the old alive. And always there is that matter of used parts; the upshot is that every living thing is a jury-rigged device.

All of which blasts the persistent rumor that Evolution seeks perfection. Evolution cares not one whit for perfection; what it cares for is refinement, sophistication, and it cares passionately for that. But there is no relationship between perfection and sophistication. The poor tuna fish bears witness.

The tuna is one of those creatures that make people lift their eyes to heaven and moan, "Here indeed is perfection—there must be a God!" and at first glance they would seem to be right. After a meticulous examination they would seem to be more right. The creature before them is probably the most sophisticated fish in the sea. Its form is a masterpiece of hydrodynamic design, its shape ideal for high speeds. Fins fit into slots and grooves; eyes lie flush with the surface of the pointed snout; finlets on the caudal declivity break up water turbulence. The tuna is a piscean missile which, in the case of the giant bluefin, can reach speeds in excess of fifty-five miles per hour, can dive or ascend a thousand feet in the space of a few minutes, and has not a concern in the world for the dangers of decompression.

The reason for these abilities is that the tunas (the seven largest species, to be precise) are warm-blooded. Astonishing as this may seem, it is true, and the advantage is clear, because warm muscle develops far more power than cold muscle. Warm-bloodedness makes for superior performance.

However, endothermy (internal heat production) in a fish is almost blasphemous to the laws of physics. The blood, which cannot help picking up great quantities of heat from the body, must pass through the gills to absorb oxygen from the sea, and gills are ideal radiators; nothing loses heat so fast as a radiator-gill. Evolution has solved this dilemma brilliantly by laying the outgoing vessels in direct contact with the incoming vessels. The outgoing vessels carry blood laden with heat; the incoming vessels carry chilled blood from its journey through the gills. So the cold blood loaded with oxygen absorbs the heat and carries it back into the body. Evolution has refined the tuna's circulatory system into an exquisite heat exchanger. It takes the place of blubber or fur.

But for all its sophistication, the tuna is still a fish. It is limited by the law of legacy, or, if you will, the law of used parts. Because water holds a mere fraction of the oxygen held in air, the only way a tuna can meet its metabolic costs is to swim fast with its mouth partially open, ramming water over the gills. Ram-gill ventilation allows a tuna to process enormous quantities of water, but here, finally, the inherent limitations of the fish catch up to sophistication. The tuna must pay a steep price for its warm blood.

In the pursuit of refinement, Evolution has jettisoned the muscles and the innervation of the gill muscles; the tuna, unlike less sophisticated fish, cannot lie stationary in the water and breathe by gulping. It must swim above a certain speed in order to meet metabolic costs. If it stops it suffocates. If it stops its body temperature also drops because the tuna generates its body warmth through exercise. Therefore, the tuna has warm blood because it swims fast; the tuna *must* swim fast because it has warm blood. The individual tuna is locked into a circular fate in which it must swim without cease, until the day it dies. The species, too, is fated to swim endlessly, for the rest of time, because it cannot go back to the ancestral motion of gulping water.

So what appears on the surface to be perfection is actually the curse of hyper-sophistication. Refinement has become, if not a liability, a relentless and onerous responsibility.

I believe that the human brain is another example of hyper-sophistication. In its blind pursuit of human percipience, Evolution has created a device which has been riddled with monumental, perhaps insurmountable, design flaws. They reveal themselves in the way that the mind embraces the world.

Perceive is the key word. The various senses send their messages along the sensory neurons in coded pulsations. The brain then interprets the code and, like a television camera, assembles a perception.

Perceptions are accurate, by and large, otherwise we could not drive down the driveway without smashing into one thing or another. But the human mind cannot leave perceptions alone. It wants to understand what the perceived thing is, how it got there, where it is going, how it fits into the world—what the world is—and this understanding seems to be the essence of *Homo sapiens*. It is central to the natural history of the species. I think that the cerebral cortex, that sublime center of cleverness, of mechanistic comprehension, must be wired into the limbic lusts. That would account for the compulsion which understanding seems to be.

But life supplies infinite perceptions, and the explanations accumulate. They accumulate until they amount to a grand explanation, a grand comprehension, of how reality works. Let us call this accretion an illusion. The mind works by creating illusions of existence.

Keep in mind that I am using the term "illusion" in the broadest sense, to include any kind of comprehension: suppositions, theories, philosophies, myths, religious beliefs, and so on, for the same method of cerebration creates them all.

Now, the interesting thing about illusions is that it doesn't seem to matter whether they are absolutely right, just so long as they are right enough that life can bumble along more or less normally. Eu-

ropeans once believed that the earth was flat, and people were secure in their illusions until Columbus went over the edge and came
back. At various times in history people have believed that malaria
is caused by bad air, that the body contains two kinds of blood,
which are separate and never mix, and as recently as the late 1950s
the scientific establishment itself believed that human beings contain forty-eight, not forty-six, chromosomes. Life went on.

What humans tolerate as normal ranges from the Eskimo's daily
duties among the icebergs to the Hottentot's coexistence with elephants, rhinoceroses, lions, mambas, to the Westerner's addiction
to televisions, computers, automobiles, fast food, unrestricted
growth and development, industrial agriculture, and fossil fuel. As
for forms of government, despite what we Americans might think,
normal government ranges from communisms, to socialisms, to oli-
garchies, dictatorships, despotisms, republics, democracies, and
variations and permutations of these, and life goes on, and the population of the world continues to rise. In the big scheme they are all
normal states of human affairs. In other words, as long as a system of
illusions stays within a remarkably permissive band of reality, you
can believe almost anything and still survive.

What does matter about illusions is that enough people buy into
the central ones, which creates internal consistency and allows
people to cooperate as a society, as a culture. And society can function quite well, apparently, in the face of wildly false illusions. Just
so long as the system of illusions operates within the wide plains of
normalcy, in other words, so long as it is benignly false, allows
people to muddle along, and does not cause out-and-out disaster,
then it will thrive. Eventually a price must be paid. There is always
a price. The society, culture, civilization will crash into reality,
which is happening to us in the West at the present time with the environmental breakdown around the planet.

The fact is, most humans are not concerned with truth; they are
concerned with political survival. If enough people share an illu-

sion, they amount to an army—of votes, if not of armed personnel. Crusades occur, mass exterminations, military buildups, as do movements in art, religion, science, philosophy—all based on the passions with which people embrace their illusions. Within each area, controversies rage and leaders fight to recruit minds for this illusion or that. This seems to be an emotional pattern that occurs in all areas of human endeavor.

And here is where, as with the tuna, the limitations of legacy overtake evolutionary refinement. The cerebral cortex sits atop the limbic system and the reptilian complex, and when all is said and decided, the rational mind serves the four F's: fleeing, fighting, feeding, etc. Evolution has used components from the monkey. This is the result.

It is compounded by the nature of mammalian learning. The ideas we learn in childhood become "imprinted" in our minds, and the normal human is not capable of and/or not interested in discarding the beliefs and values acquired in childhood. Life is too short. There is too much to lose. There is too much anxiety, too many chances to fail in starting over.

Evolution has solved this dilemma with one of its most brilliant inventions. It is known as denial, the bodyguard of false illusion. *Homo sapiens* possesses an absolutely fabulous ability to deny the truth. And why not. If a man has twenty million dollars in blue chip stocks, a mountain chalet, a yacht, several wives in sequence, and various kids, he has proven his fitness in the prevailing system. He has won mates, territory, a good position on the peck order—in short, he has satisfied the demands of his limbic system and his reptilian complex. He is not about to question the illusions under which he has earned all this.

And so we come to the ultimate test of the human mind: the salvation of the environment. Can *Homo sapiens* survive the threat of itself? In light of its capacity for false illusion and its phenomenal capacity for denial, can it even conceive the issues?

The master switches are population growth and Western economics. There is no unified, enforceable, worldwide policy to deal with them, and they are diametrically opposed to long-term survival. Five billion people cannot help but poison the earth's physiology, because five billion mouths devour so much of the planet's biomass that the ecosystems are shorted, and five billion anuses produce so much feces that unless it is all recycled through the soil in which it originated, it accumulates in the water tables or in the offshore waters. Five billion people also desire the comfortable, easy, painless, narcotic lifestyle of the West, and that limbic desire foments Western industry. The living surface of Earth is a biological organ and cannot survive the caustic feces that industry for five billion produces. And Western economics, based on indefinite growth and driven by the self-interest of each individual, begets hysterical consumption of resources.

Yet at the present time there is no political or religious movement with the remotest chance of defeating the illusions that be. The masses of *Homo sapiens* deny that anything is ill with their world. Ozone holes, greenhouse effects, desertification, fouling of aquifers, erosion of soil, pesticide treadmills, extermination of fisheries, buildup of toxic and nuclear wastes, accumulation of garbage, an extinction rate equal to that caused by the last asteroid—the corporate heads and the heads of state declare they are leading us toward the light, that Mother Earth will always provide, that the gods will always intervene. Whole books are written in defense of this thesis, sophisticated books armed with the most refined rationalizations. The illusions, I fear, will remain false until the reality crumbles.

Which brings us back to Evolution and its fondness for refining the old in pursuit of sophistication, not perfection. How sublime the human mind, how exquisite the reasoning center and the power of rationalization. How utterly flawed its essence.

For those who seek the truth, I suspect it is something like this: as

Evolution attempted with the tuna, it has made a rousing attempt to lift *Homo sapiens* above its legacy. But try as Evolution will, the species will always be mammalian. No matter how sophisticated its "higher" faculties become, it will always be the ultimate in the sophisticated monkey. It will never transcend the inherent limitations of its ancestral parts. In the end it finds itself performing the same kind of flawed circular fate as the tuna: *Homo sapiens* deceives itself because of the ancestry of its brain; because of the ancestry of its brain, *Homo sapiens must* deceive itself.

And what has all this to do with my cockroach memoirs? It is all context, my friends—background to illuminate what the roaches taught me in the rearing room. Evolution, despite its compulsion to refine, does stumble close to perfection from geologic time to geologic time. The cockroach is as near to perfection as Evolution has ever come.

Since the basic goal of evolution is survival, perfection would be eternal existence. By that criterion the cockroach is approaching the ultimate end; it has been around in recognizable form for at least 320 million years. The basic purpose of the brain is to aid survival. By *that* criterion the cockroach is divine genius, and *Homo sapiens*, which has been around for about 40 thousand years, does not appear to be a very bright creature. It is another result of Evolution's flawed character.

It has been fifteen years now since I studied the cockroach. Like all humans who live in cities, I do on occasion run into these insects, and I must confess that whenever I do, those old lessons come to life.

I was jogging at night, several months ago, when I fell into a pothole and broke my right ankle. Shock set in, and not realizing the bone was fractured, I began limping to the nearest telephone booth to call home for a ride. No sooner did I set out, however, than I spotted a cat crouched on a manhole cover. Sure enough, a fat American roach came feeling its way up through the tool hole. The cat, the tip of its tail twitching, tensed and aimed. It pounced, cuffed the insect about, pinned it down, and grabbed it in its mouth.

I moved closer and saw another roach searching for food. Just for the hell of it, I shooed it toward the cat. The cat could not resist a moving roach and dropped the first to pursue the second. The first roach skittered hysterically for a few feet, slowed to a walk, and stopped still as a stone. The cat, now holding the second roach in its jaws, crouched in the street and stared suspiciously at me. I stood gingerly on one foot and stared back, the four of us fixed motionless in the blackness. Then the first roach turned back toward the man-hole, the cat dropped the second roach to grab the first, and I hobbled off to get medical aid. It felt like the logical thing to do.

PART II

ALFALFA

COMMUNION

It's a jubilant day along the mid-California coast. A storm is breaking up, and the cloud armada proceeds majestically southward, under sail and before the wind. From below, their hulls are broad and dark and their prows blunt, but the sails billow upward for thousands of feet and catch a river of wind that collects in the calyx of the Monterey bight and funnels into the Salinas Valley. With the sun standing at a little past noon, the Santa Lucia Mountains glower dark and ominous to the west of the valley, a massive wall in shadow; the Gabilan Mountains lie in the sun to the east, foothills clothed in freshly sprouting grass and rising in lumps to the peaks farther back. Huge shadows race along the ground, contradicting the illusion that the cloud galleons move slowly. It's astonishing how quickly a mile of darkness passes over the land.

It has been a wet spring, and the fields are moist and black. Infant lettuces, broccolis, cauliflowers, and brussels sprouts sit in mile-long furrows. The temperature is about 55°F, and air is charging south at forty to fifty miles per hour in cold, stinging gusts. The alfalfa falls down in waves of silvery prostration.

I am driving to the small town of Gonzales, fifteen miles south of

Salinas. There, in the right-angle turn of Old Stage Road, the same road the Wells Fargo coaches once traveled, is nestled the dairy farm of one John DaOro, his two brothers, and their mother. The county agent has contacted the DaOros, and they have agreed to let me run experiments on a corner of their northwest alfalfa field.

I intend to study the induction of diapause (hibernation) in *Bathyplectes curculionis*, a larval parasite of the immature alfalfa weevil, *Hypera brunneipennis*. In plain language, I am trying to figure out what makes a little wasp hibernate. I am going to become a scientist, and this is my dissertation research.

The wasp is known only by its scientific name, *Bathyplectes curculionis* (pronounced ƀath-ee-ṕlec-teez cur-ƙool-ee-áhn-is); it is called a parasite because it lays its eggs inside the larvae of the alfalfa weevil. In reality, *Bathyplectes* is a predator, because when the egg hatches, the wasp larva starts to consume the contents of its host's body. It eats slowly, developing gradually to maintain its vehicle while it itself matures. It even waits until the weevil grub spins its cocoon; then, in a metabolic sprint, the wasp completes its growth and consumes the remainder of the weevil's carcass. This strategy of the lethal fetus is completely normal in the insect world; indeed, parasitic predators are the only force that stands between us and a world consumed by plant-eating insects. (Parasitic insects inspired the monster in the movie *Alien*.)

After they have killed their hosts, the young wasps spin a chocolate-brown cocoon the size of a rice grain, girthed by a white belt. Then they hibernate, or, as we say in entomology, "diapause." Their metabolism slows almost to a stop, and they can now cope with cold, heat, dryness, and lack of food.

So, what triggers this state of arrested metabolism? That is what I aim to find out. The wasps need some sort of environmental cue to tell their physiology when to store fat and when to prepare for metabolic shutdown. In many insects, day length is the ideal time cue, for it does not depend on the local idiosyncrasies of seasonal temperature. I will test this possibility; but temperature, too, can play a part, so I must gather information on the temperatures in the alfalfa itself. I will need continuous records for one year.

I will study these insects in the field and in the laboratory. I will put them in special chambers in which I can control the photophase and the scotophase—how long the lights are on and off—and I will control the temperature. Insects are wonderful subjects, such accommodating units, such oblivious little pieces. No intellect at all. You just turn on the experiment without any feelings of remorse or guilt and see what happens. Data. Statistics. Computer analyses.

The back of the university station wagon is loaded with scientific instruments for recording temperature, humidity, day length, and sunlight; insect nets and cages; tool boxes; and an official Stevenson Screen weather shelter—a standardized white box with ventilated walls designed to protect scientific instruments from direct sunlight and vandals. I will assemble it in DaOro's field, and each week I will drive the 125 miles south from Berkeley and service the recorders, change the recording sheets, refill the ink pens.

I pull off Highway 101, head north on Old Stage Road, and stop at the alfalfa field a quarter-mile east of the right-angle crook. DaOro is sitting on an old John Deere tractor. A man of medium height and build, he is wearing a ragged ski jacket and a light-blue tennis hat, the floppy kind with a two-inch rim all the way around. The wind has chapped his high-bridged Italian nose and given a blush to his cheeks. He sits with his right arm draped over the wheel, watching quizzically as I climb from the station wagon.

"Hi. You John DaOro?"

"Yeah. You the guy from the university?"

"Yeah. Sorry I'm so late."

"Oh, no problem. I live here. I have plenty to do."

I can't stanch the guilt welling up inside. There is no sarcasm in his voice; he really does have plenty to do, and he assumes that I am an adult and must have good reasons for being late. His voice has a surprising lilt to it.

We shake hands and I begin to explain what I'm doing there. I am a graduate student at the University of California and . . . what? What do I think of the principle of free speech? Well, I'm not really too keen on just how free it got. In the university you somehow come to believe that all farmers are red-necked conservatives. But he says he sees their side. Whatever his persuasions, I like his manner.

We continue to talk. We talk about the farming policies of the secretary of agriculture. We talk about the psychology of immigration—his parents came here from the Italian sector of Switzerland. We talk about animal training and alfalfa culture and morality as a practical psychological mechanism. Two hours go by and still we stand by Old Stage Road, knee deep in alfalfa, the wind blowing our hair every which way, our arms whirling and pumping with great gusto—talking. Finally the conversation comes back to the Free Speech Movement, which reminds John DaOro of an incident.

"The other day I was driving south on 101 and I saw these two hippies hitchhiking. Why do they look like that? They were so dirty and bedraggled. They looked so unhappy."

"Well, what'd you do?"

"I gave them a ride."

"You did!? Why'd you do *that*?"

"Well, I wanted to know why they looked like that. I wanted to understand how they felt."

He faces into the wind and gives a little shrug, turning arms out slightly in a gentle, honest gesture. "I love this valley. I love being a farmer. Look at those mountains. Feel this soil. The wind, the sun, the plants, the animals. I love being alive. I just wanted to know what their reason was for looking so unhappy."

Acceptance: What a remarkable trait to have. To exist and not feel compelled to judge. To forget the importance of self.

Finally we get down to the business of setting up shop. DaOro is genuinely interested in the various instruments, and he seems to understand the technical terms. If he doesn't understand, he asks. The temperature down in the alfalfa fascinates him. It fascinates me, too, and soon I am explaining how each of the instruments works and how to interpret the ink-line recordings.

"The alfalfa is a carpet, John, and the stems are the pile. Down there in that carpet a miniature climate is going on, and it has a beat, a pulse. The temperature rises in the day and falls at night, up and down, up and down. It's like jazz; the rhythm is always changing, never repeating the day before, always a subtle variation. The instruments? They're recording the score. They're taking down the music of the field, and we can play it again by following the graph line."

"Why are you doing all this?"

DaOro has just stepped onto dangerous ground. Dissertation research is the whole world to a graduate student. Ask him to explain that world and you are in for an exhausting experience. Before I explain the theories of diapause, I have to explain the context, about all the creatures that live in a field of alfalfa—all the one thousand–plus species counted so far. I cannot help myself. I open the mental textbooks I've had to memorize and the words gush out. Not just facts about insects, but facts about all the other arthropods—the arachnids, the isopods, the diplopods, the chilopods, the pauropods—that share the field.

"Hey, Bill," DaOro cuts me off. "Have you actually *seen* these things?"

"Well, not all of them. But *most* of them."

"Come on. I want to *see* these things you're talking about."

I get the feeling that I have been misled about farmers and victimized by preconceived notions. For a fraction of a second I glimpse the hulk of a more ponderous thought—that preconceived notions are the basis of modern science, for what is education but the imposition on open young minds of the observations, insights, hypotheses, theories, and philosophies of others? It is all second hand. It is knowledge gained cheap, without having to earn it through direct, dirty experience. It is prejudice—institutionalized, unavoidable, and largely necessary, but prejudice nonetheless.

The thought disappears as quickly as it loomed; it will return someday, when I am more suited by experience to handle it. DaOro nods his head toward the field, I nod back, pick up my sweep net and my tool chest of forceps, thermometers, shell vials, insect aspirators, and other tools of the entomologist's trade, and join him.

We wade out into the thick, dense green. The field is just entering its second year, and the plants are at the height of their vigor—about a foot and a half tall with succulent, crisp stems. They rustle like tossed lettuce as our boots tear through. A hundred yards from the road, DaOro suggests we stop; this is about as pure as alfalfa gets.

But the wind is now biting into us. The sun is still shining and the cloud galleons are still soaring past, but they are closer together, as if massing for another battle. Their shadows slip silently across the valley floor, caressing the land. After several hours of standing in the open, we are chilled. Our jackets are zipped up to our chins. I wouldn't mind walking some more, just to drive back the shivers.

I bend over and push the plants apart, looking for the first insect that strikes my eye.

"What are you doing, Bill?"

"Looking for insects. You wanted to see insects, didn't you?"

"Come on, Bill, you can't look for insects like that. Do it like this . . ."

DaOro drops to all fours, rolls onto his left side, and disappears. A half-hour ago I would have smiled patronizingly at a suggestion like this. We don't learn such techniques in graduate work, but somehow it makes sense. Then I am on all fours, and then I am lying on my right side, and then the two of us are lying head to head in the alfalfa field.

We find ourselves in an alternate reality. There is no wind down here, only air. It is balmy, about 75°F; it feels as though we have lowered ourselves into warm water. I stick my head up for a moment to make sure I am still planted in reality, and there, just as before, is the alfalfa sea stretching flat and pure for a half-mile south and east. The wind is still blasting, astringent and cold, no more than two feet above us. But as I lower my head again, I descend into the Amazon basin.

For a moment I am disoriented. My eyes strain to focus on stems and leaves and blossoms a foot or two in front of my face. At first they are simply a blur of green. Then details begin to form.

The resemblance to a rain forest is striking. Each plant grows from the ground in a long, straight stem. About a foot above the surface it branches out, ending in clusters of leaves, leaves and stems weave a canopy with the stems and leaves of the nearby plants. The ground itself is relatively bare, also like in a rain forest.

All I see, however, is alfalfa. I know that animal life exists, but I don't see any.

"Hey, Bill, what's this!?"

DaOro points at something on the soft, tender tissue just below a bud. It is the shape of an egg, but tiny, about an eighth-inch long. Pale green and translucent, like a tiny grape, it blends perfectly with its surroundings. Two pipes protrude like anti-aircraft guns from its rump; two long, graceful antennae arch back from its head over its back; and two bulbous eyes stare in all directions like hemispherical gun turrets. A tubular snout, projecting from the bottom of its face, appears to be embedded in the plant tissue between its legs.

"That's a pea aphid, *Acyrthosiphon pisum*."

DaOro leans closer. "So that's what they look like up close. Hey, they're really neat! Two years ago we had to spray for them, but I had no idea they looked like this."

Suddenly another aphid seems to materialize just above the first, and another just below, and others to each side, and as if a new slide has been projected on a screen, the mind suddenly grasps a new reality: The end of the branch is clothed in pea aphids! They look like an ankle warmer of furry green.

"Look at the little ones!" says DaOro.

This is something I am familiar with, since my duties have included such tasks as rearing aphids in the insectary in order to breed aphid parasites. I explain to DaOro that most aphids bear live young during most of the breeding season and all are female. They are parthenogenetic and do not require males in order to conceive. Within the week the young females are producing their own young, and if you prepare mature female aphids for microscopic examination, you can sometimes see embryos forming. Parthenogenesis is a reproductive strategy that, by eliminating courtship, mating, and subsequent gestation time, elevates the rate of reproduction to astronomic levels. Aphids lie at the base of the food pyramid, they provide food for countless predators, and their strategy is to offset predatory losses with a deluge of newborn.

Even as I talk, DaOro is looking closer still, and we both react to the aphids at the same time. For here and there in this protoplasmic cluster are aphids with their rumps raised high into the air, and emerging from the ends are tiny, tiny babies. They look and move exactly like minuscule calves. They are coming into the world head first. One of them has actually freed itself from its maternal bond and is doddering about on unsteady legs. We are both about one foot away from the colony at this point, both peering intently.

"What's this thing?" DaOro points to a slender, tan insect that looks like a very small mantis but has a proboscis extending backward and tucked into a groove on its belly. I flip through the pages of my mental textbook.

"I think that's a damsel bug," I announce tentatively. "It's supposed to be a predator, but I don't know what it eats."

"Maybe pea aphids?" suggests DaOro.

"Yeah, but it may eat insect eggs, too."

"What's that brown thing with the long nose?"

"Aha! An alfalfa weevil. That's one of the things I'll be studying."

"Look at that snout!" says DaOro. "What's it used for? It must be used for something."

This is one of the basic tenets of ecology, ethology, and evolution theory: the structure reflects the purpose. (It is also a tenet of common sense, which should lie at the core of science anyway.) The weevil's snout amounts to about one-third of the body length and looks like a very long nose. Two clublike antennae protrude to each side just before the snout's tip and look, from our gross perspective, like a pair of spectacles. The snout operates as a drill—jaws at the end of a shaft—with which the weevil bores through the walls of alfalfa stems to lay clusters of orange-yellow eggs in the hollow interior. It also bores into the buds and gets the freshest, tenderest cuts of botanical flesh.

Gradually we forget our conscious selves, curiosity transcending substance, and merge with a feeling of the field. It is a parallel universe, and it swarms with living things. Everywhere we look, creatures stare back, little gargoyles and griffins and goblins. Spittle bugs encased in pods of foam; buffalo treehoppers with great spines jutting from each shoulder, eyes on the sides of a wide green head; tiny black pirate bugs, their white wings folded like napkins across their backs; big-eyed bugs like miniature frogs; caterpillars with black bodies and yellow stripes; green inchworms that measure as they walk; spiders lurking in their silken tunnels which open out onto their cloth verandas—they are everywhere, the tortured imagination of Hieronymus Bosch made manifest, sitting impassively on the leaves, clinging warily to the undersides of leaves, wedged into axils where the branches meet.

Looking like a miniature red helmet, a lady beetle crawls along a branch, over the leaves, under the leaves, searching for pea aphids. Another red helmet is pinning a victim on its back; green legs flail in the air as the beetle eats. Crawling up another plant is a lacewing larva—an alien creature indeed. About a quarter-inch long, its shape suggests an alligator, scaly lumps lining its back. But instead of a snout, it has a pair of needle-sharp pincers which extend forward at least one-quarter of its body length. This miniature monster is foraging for aphids, mites, insect eggs—anything nontoxic that it can overpower. It poles its body along by reaching forward with its abdomen, gripping the surface with an adhesive gland on the abdominal tip, and pushing backward. It scurries blindly, groping its way, and finally runs into the aphid colony. Without pausing it grabs an aphid in its pincers, hoists it into the air, and begins to suck the life out of its body. This larva, when it matures and hatches into an adult, will become the exquisite green lacewing, a fragile, nectar-and-pollen-seeking insect with cellophane wings and golden eyes.

Another Boschian predator comes groping up the alfalfa stem: a blind, green maggot, which tapers from a wide, blunt rear to a flexible, headless point. Like the lacewing larva, it also grasps the plant with an adhesive gland on its rump. But after each hike forward, this creature gropes from side to side like someone feeling around in the dark for a dropped coin. It, too, encounters the colony. The aphids seem to sense its arrival. They thrust their abdomens into the air and wag back and forth. Globules of a white, viscous fluid seem to inflate like balloons on the ends of the two tail pipes with which each aphid is equipped. This is a noxious liquid that repels parasitic wasps, but has no effect on this headless horror. The maggot strikes like a snake: Two hooks emerge from its throat, then the slender, pointed anterior end plucks a big, succulent aphid from the group, hoists it high, and, again like the lacewing larva, sucks the fluids from its prey. This grotesque predator will transform into the sublime creature known as a hover fly, which hangs motionless in air for minutes at a time flaunting its red eyes and its black-and-yellow body.

Then I see something special. I nudge DaOro and point.

"There it is, John—my guy, without which I will not become a scientist."

DaOro peers at a creature the size of a mosquito that is clearly a wasp. It is standing with trance-like stillness on a bud of alfalfa. Only its antennae move, waving back and forth in slow motion. It is *Bathyplectes curculionis*, a healthy young female, and she is a beauty. Black and shiny as volcanic glass, this little lady has stylish tastes. She wears yellow sleeves on each of her six legs, and on the underside of her abdomen she sports a yellow apron. Yellow on black; it is a stunning combination.

"What is that thing sticking from its rear?" asks DaOro in a hushed voice, fearful of breathing on her.

"The ovipositor," I whisper back. "The egg-layer." It attaches under the tip of her abdomen and extends backward one third of her body length, curving slightly upward like the saber it is. I explain, taking care not to alarm her with breath, that what we see is actually the scabbard, for the blade itself is sheathed inside. As in all wasps, the egg-laying tool has been conscripted for double duty as a stinger; in the parasitic wasps, it is used as a syringe to insert eggs into the prey.

She stirs. Reaching forward with her antennae, she begins to palpate the surface of the bud. Tension vibrates back along the bowed antenna shafts to her head. She flips her wings nervously, a repetitious tic, and then sets off at a quick trot to hunt.

Holding her antennae forward, the tips bowed down, she pats the plant as she scurries along, divining the scent of her quarry. Out one branch, over the terminal, back to the main trunk, touching, feeling, smelling. Up along the main trunk, out along another branch.

Suddenly she senses something. The antennae probe urgently between the surfaces of the stem and the immature leaves wrapped around the terminal bud. Then she stands up to her full height on all six legs, arches her abdomen, and swings the ovipositor down into position; the blade emerges from the end of the sheath and she jabs repeatedly between the leaves of the bud.

"It has taste buds on the end!" I hiss at DaOro. DaOro nods. We both strain to see the object of her attentions, but at first we cannot. Then, wedged between the leaf and the bud, we spot it: a succulent green grub with a brown head, a yellow stripe running down its quarter-inch length. It is a fourth-instar larva of the alfalfa weevil; it has shed its skin three times and is in the fourth and final growth period.

The point of the jabbing ovipositor comes closer, closer. The larva somehow senses the danger and begins to wriggle free from the bud. Rising up, it waves its head and body wildly and blindly, trying to strike the foe. Without hesitation the wasp moves in, stabbing like a sewing machine in the direction of the larva. Finally its stinger touches fat green flesh. With a great abdominal heave, the wasp drives the blade deep into the larva's body, just behind the head.

The larva convulses; its entire body lashes back and forth. Each contortion tosses the wasp by its stinger, bashing its body against leaves, stems, buds. The pair wrestle and writhe, the larval weevil fighting for its life, the wasp for the future of its genes. But the stinger remains in place while a soft, malleable egg emerges from the stinger shaft. Bathed in the larva's colorless blood and massaged by coiling viscera, the egg assumes the natural form of a stout sausage. It awaits its hatching several days hence.

Its mission accomplished, the wasp jerks its stinger from the larva's neck. A large drop of digestive fluid bubbles from the larva's mouth, and it crawls off, stopping every few seconds to lash out in anger, raging in its sub-rational way against the devil seed planted in the womb of its own tissues. The battle has taken about four seconds.

The wasp now celebrates. She draws herself up to full height, flexes her wings and folds them over her back, drops her antennae, and stands there twitching. Finally calmed, she turns to the task of personal hygiene. Standing on her first two pairs of legs, she reaches over her back with her hindlegs and strokes backward time and again, combing dirt and other debris from her wings and abdomen. Minutes are spent on the abdomen and wings, then comes the head.

Now she stands on her middle and hind legs and reaches up with her forelegs. She grasps one antennae between her "wrist" and a special thumblike grooming spine. The grip forms a perfectly shaped opening through which she now draws the antenna, lifting up at the base like a fisherman straining against a fish. After each antenna is thoroughly scraped she rubs her face and head, reaching back and stroking downward. The motion is identical to the motion of a grooming cat.

The toilette takes five minutes, maybe ten. Time is vague in the realm of alfalfa. When she has finished, she walks quickly to the top of the bud, tenses, raises her wings, springs into dizzy, uncontrolled flight, and disappears among the stems and leaves. This style of flight is designed to catapult the wasp at random between plants, there being no need for directed flight in such tight quarters. The goal is to save the time and energy of walking from one alfalfa branch to another via the main stem. At any rate, she has parted company with us; our clearing in the alfalfa forest seems somehow empty.

DaOro then nudges me and points to a place about eighteen inches away. There she stands, cleaning her antennae with alternating strokes of her front legs while clinging to a cluster of alfalfa blossoms. She radiates joy, and we feel surrounded by life again.

The blossoms add to our pleasure. Tiny trumpets of lavender are inserted side by side around the stem, each flaring out from the center like the bristles of a brush. She scurries up to the clustered blossoms, pauses to examine one of the florets with her antennae, then plunges her head and shoulders into the floral throat. With just the tips of her antennae protruding from within and her ovipositor raised into the air, she drinks deep of the nectar. She holds this pose for several minutes. Finally she backs out, strokes her head a few times, vibrates her wings to heat her flight muscles, and springs aloft. We try to follow her path, but she heads into the dense tangle of the alfalfa jungle and is gone. This time there is no doubt.

Our eyes meet and we know that the enchantment has come to an end. Stiffly we get up on all fours, then stand slowly upright. Higher and higher we rise, and as we rise the jungle closes over, transformed once again into a green field. We continue to rise until we stand fully erect, into the wind, into the jet stream of our own dimension.

We trudge slowly across the field. I pack my gear and thank DaOro for his time and the good company. I do not thank him for the most stimulating conversation I have had in months, nor do I mention the natural élan with which he has punctured my arrogance. Besides, I know that he knows anyway. We wave, I climb into the station wagon, turn onto Old Stage Road, then north onto Highway 101, and drive into the wind. The sun has descended behind the ominous wall of the Santa Lucias; as the evening comes, the clouds grow darker and sail closer together, the fields grow blacker, and the wind rushes in faster from the sea.

I will go back to Berkeley, and I will endure the intellectual gamut of the graduate curriculum. I will study my little *Bathyplectes* in the lab, caging her in plastic boxes, subjecting her to different combinations of day length and temperature, and I will present the findings in the proper scientific format. But somehow the grail of science is no longer so important.

THE

STRANGE CASE

OF THE

ELECTRIC RAY

INTRODUCTION, MATERIALS AND METHODS, AND REVELATIONS

Richard Bray is a big, kindly, affable man in his late forties. He is tanned, with a bit of gray at the temples and a dusting in his hair, and he teaches marine biology at Long Beach State University. The years have been kind to Richard Bray, in part, I suspect, because he loves teaching young people about the workings of fish and seaweed and rocky grottoes and sponges and corals; he also loves the work of finding these marine things out, of stroking through the water in fins, carrying his air and his life in tanks strapped to his back, reveling all the while in a world beneath the waves, completely devoid of humans. Consequently, his spirit is young and enthusiastic, and his eyes open wide as a boy's when he addresses you. He still laughs over his first encounter with the human side of science, the kind of en-counter that has made lesser men bitter. This is how it happened.

One day about fifteen years ago, when Bray was a young graduate student at the University of California at Santa Barbara, he went diving with some friends. He was just swimming along slowly, mind-ing his own business, reveling in the beauty of the wavering, aqua-marine light, when something soft and gentle, like a floating rag, settled on his head. Before he could react, a tremendous, walloping ZAP stunned him. This was followed by a second one, slightly weaker. And a third, weaker still.

That was Bray's introduction to the California electric ray, *Tor-pedo californica*.

"I don't know if it ran out of gas or it just lost interest in me," Bray says now, "and I'm not in the habit of sticking my finger in electric sockets, but from what I remember as a kid that's what it felt like."

It was a small individual, about five pounds, and Bray's reference to an electric socket is quite apt. A ray of that size can generate around sixty volts and ten amps, about half the standard household current. That's impressive enough, but consider the fact that Cali-fornia electric rays grow to more than four feet in length, reach a weight of more than ninety pounds, and generate energy in propor-tion to their size; this scales up to a shock of several hundred volts.

"I guess it's accurate to say that that experience increased my in-terest in them," says Bray.

As time went on he began to make mental notes and to learn more about these residents of the California coast. And remarkable creatures they turned out to be. Everything from their external ap-pearance to their internal wiring is unique. An average adult is sev-eral feet long, weighs about twenty or thirty pounds, and has the tail and skin of a shark (its close relative). In front of the tail the body expands into a wide, circular disk, like batter poured on a griddle; the eyes are set on the top of this disk, and the mouth is inserted on the white underside. But the oddest and most impressive attribute is the electric organs, which were located in the disk. They account for about 15 percent of the body's weight.

At the time, the ray's habits were not well known. They were said to be sluggish creatures, which lay on the bottom, buried themselves in the sand, and used their zappers to discourage aggression.

Several years after his encounter, Bray, assisted by fellow student Mark Hixon, began a nighttime study of Naples Reef off the city of Santa Barbara. With his heightened awareness of rays, Bray realized that they must be creatures of the night. He saw an average of two per dive. Not only that, but they were actively swimming, and Bray got the definite impression that they were foraging for food. The impression was soon borne out by one of those events to which the chosen are privy.

Once again Bray and Hixon were swimming along one night, when they spotted a thirty-inch ray swimming directly toward them. "As you might expect," says Bray, "we started backing up." The ray kept advancing. At the same time, it inclined its body at a forty-five-degree angle, exposing its pale underside, which became a dazzling white disk in the glare of the diving lights.

The ray swam menacingly closer. Bray and Hixon backpedaled vigorously. And then a fourth player arrived on the scene.

Maybe it was drawn to the disk of white glaring against the deep blackness; maybe it swam up from behind to investigate, passed before the lights, and was blinded. Whatever the reason, it wriggled past and wobbled erratically toward the ray—an eight-inch jack mackerel.

Bray and Hixon watched with relief as the poor innocent came between them and the threat, and they were completely unprepared for what happened next. Just as the mackerel and the ray were about to collide, the ray lunged forward with a powerful stroke of its tail, ducked its head into a forward roll, and in one continuous motion cupped its body around the mackerel, like the palm of a huge, fingerless hand. Continuing its roll, the ray reached the nadir of its arc, belly toward the night sky. The mackerel's body quivered. Its eyes bulged. Its fins stood stiff and erect. Its lips protruded, and its mouth gaped in a silent cry. It was gripped in the palm of doom, and Bray knew exactly how it felt.

The dance continued. The ray completed its roll, and as it did, the edges of its body began to undulate, wave upon wave traveling from back to front, nudging the embraced mackerel into position under the ray's mouth. It gulped twice, three times, and the fish was gone. The entire event, from attack to finish, took less than ten seconds.

Bray was elated. He had seen with his own eyes how the ray used its electric charge, and it was clearly a predatory device. Sharks, barracudas, dolphins, and the vast majority of marine predators use teeth for the kill; these rays used electricity. Furthermore, he had proof: Hixon had had the presence of mind to photograph the entire event. All that remained was to write up the findings, send them off to some scientific journal, and reap a bit of well-deserved praise for setting the facts straight. That's the way science works.

Bray finished the paper and sent it to *Science*, the most prestigious journal in the American scientific establishment. Now, when a scientific journal receives a submission, the custom is to send the paper to other experts in the same field of research. There is no option but to choose workers in the same field, because science has refined itself into such remote, convoluted, codified, code-deified sanctums of left-brain penance that no one but a second expert can understand what the first is saying, and this is not an exaggeration. The referees critique the new paper, give it their professional seal of approval, and, by doing so, are supposed to ensure that scientific standards blow on high in the clear air of truth.

Bray's paper came back rejected almost by return post. One of his reviewers felt that Bray should "tone down" his claims, that he "really didn't have any direct evidence."

Bray was incredulous. "If you look at that photograph, if you look at that jack mackerel . . . something *happened* to it—they just don't hang around like that!" But after the incredulity wore off, his combative spirit took over, and he met the challenge.

"We were a bunch of young graduate students," says Bray, "and we figured, 'Hell, we *know* they're predators—let's just *demonstrate* it!'"

Rarely are demonstrations so elegant and sweet, or so ingenious. Using a shower curtain ring, Bray made a clamp to hold a small fish. He glued the clamp to the end of a long, thin fiberglass pole. Then he fixed a camera flashbulb to the clamp. And *then* he and Hixon went out into the black nighttime waters over Naples Reef.

They soon spotted a ray in the light of the diving lamps. Swimming as close as seemed prudent, Bray baited the device, handed it to Hixon, and turned off the lights. Hixon, holding the rod before him like a sword, groped through the black water toward the spot where he had last seen the ray. Bray opened the shutter on his camera and pointed it in the same direction. They waited. Nothing happened. Hixon edged closer, millimetrically, a man swimming among mines. Breath hissed through their regulators; bubbles streamed up toward the surface.

And then: There was light, there was truth, there was proof. There was Hixon, suspended in that split, existential second, holding the pole. The ray was cupped over the fish, the fish was frozen in the throes of electric tetany, and the flashbulb glowed through the ray's flesh. "Let There Be Light" commands the motto of the University of California, and Bray had taken the commandment literally. In what is still admired as a classic experiment, he had let the ray bring the batteries, so to speak, and tricked it into firing the flash and taking its own picture in the process.

The evidence was unassailable. The California electric ray packed enough voltage to use as a predatory weapon. It displayed what appeared to be a predatory inclination. Therefore, concluded sicence, it *probably* is an electric predator. Bray sent the picture off, and a week later the editor called to say his paper had been accepted.

DISCUSSION, CONCLUSIONS, ETC.

I think about that scene now and then. I think about the truth and beauty of its revelation. I thrill to its *rightness*, to the elegance and finality of Bray's simple proof. It is knowing on the deepest, most visceral level, where axons deliver direct experience from the eye unto the brain and the corpus callosum bridges image and comprehension back and forth, left to right, right to left, in the architecture of the mind. Reason fuses with feeling, transcends intellect, mingles with the spirit of existence. Then I think about the process of scientific acceptance, the process by which revelation is reduced to fact.

There is no question that science draws its monolithic strength from the enshrinement of skepticism. Observations must be questioned. Experiments must be repeated by other scientists, and the results must match. It is an agenda that irons out the wrinkles of self-delusion from the perceptions of *Homo sapiens*. But, like all social actions, it inevitably leads to collisions of ego, and collisions hurt. Science can be a painful and angry endeavor; yet science is supposed to be above all that. It is the realm of the rational mind. It is supposed to float in an aerial zone high above the torments of normal life. That, however, is an illusion. The process of science cannot operate without its psychological cuts and bruises. As a matter of fact, the success of science is probably due as much to negative emotions and negative motives as it is to cleverness.

This is how the process works: a scientist writes according to the style and form of a scientific article—introduction, materials and methods, results, discussion, conclusions. He sends it to a professional journal, which in turn sends it to various peers for critique.

And the moment it is clutched in a peer's palm it begins its journey down into a labyrinth of academic principalities, territorial rejoinders, self-interests, petty jealousies, and the hierarchies of dominance called peck orders. It has entered the basement of science—namely, politics.

The peers chosen for the task of review and critique usually dwell in the same research territory; in other words, they are competitors. Your revelation is delivered for judgment into the hands of your rivals! Can a more critical, biased, and self-invested jury be found? Older, more established scientists, those who rank higher in the peck order and have allies or favors owed in the right places, can see their offerings ushered into friendlier hands. But the young idealists, the students nurtured at the teat of scientific philosophy—well, they leap into the cold, black water of Naples Reef when they submit that first revelation to their peers, as my friend Bray found out.

But suppose the paper is accepted, and eventually, after confirmation, so are its facts and notions. Let us talk for a moment about the fallibility of scientific knowledge.

Once a fact or notion is accepted, once it is cemented into the great cathedral of science, it is very difficult to remove. The longer it lies undisturbed, the deeper it gets buried beneath the sediment of subsequent facts. More theory is built upon it, more books based upon it, more of civilization erected upon it. More careers stand to be rumpled should a "fact" be dislodged. Anyone who questions, much less challenges, is therefore laying siege to the edifice and had better have good evidence and good allies.

In Bray's case, the electric ray as merely a high-voltage slug was a minor notion whose disabuse had little impact on the scientific world. Yet it still took defiance, determination, perseverance, and supererogatory evidence to prove the obvious. Maybe that's as it should be—survival of the fit. But it is still a disillusioning jolt the first few times a scientist runs into this schizophrenic side of the scientific process. On the one hand, the idylls of discovery, the quiet, innocent explorations of Dr. Jekyll; on the other, the tensions of combat, the anger, the spite, the envy, the vengeful machinations of Mr. Hyde.

And so it is. Established science looms over the scientists who practice it, and all but the naive and the brave are inhibited. This acceptance serves to shield the fallacies and misconceptions that lie embedded like fossils in the edifice, ossified in acceptance and protected by the status quo.

However, science has an adequate supply of both the naive and the brave, and now and then one of them will chisel into the wall on some innocent exploration. Suddenly a big chunk will break off, and there will lie one of these erroneous items exposed to light and air for the first time in years. The entire edifice of science will then tremble. Such an event occurred when I was in high school at the start of the 1960s.

I had gone home for the summer vacation at the end of my junior year believing that I had forty-eight chromosomes in each cell. All human beings did, we were taught; it was simply an Absolute Truth. If you said forty-seven or forty-nine, or anything but forty-eight, you were wrong. The number forty-eight was considered fundamental and sacrosanct.

I went home that summer just bouncing with enthusiasm, secure in the knowledge that I had forty-eight of those little clickers inside each of my quadrillion-odd cells, all snapping their molecular fingers, each snap striking a minuscule spark in the metabolic cosmos of my consciousness. But when I returned for my senior year, I found out that the unspeakable had happened: I had lost two chromosomes. I now had forty-six.

What happened, of course, was that someone had sat down and counted. Oh, how he must have counted through that microscopic circle of light, backward and forward, forward and backward, inside out and outside in. And all he found was forty-six. Imagine the task of reprinting all those biology texts, of reconfiguring the minds of

Western civilization, all of whom had been taught forty-eight. Imagine the resistance to a discovery like that.

History is a monument to scientific revolutions like this. History is dedicated to recording the errors of the past, and it is replete with examples: the earth is flat, the earth is round; the earth is the center of the universe, the earth revolves around the sun; disease is caused by bodily humors that fall out of balance, disease is caused by microbes—and on and on, each age embracing its notions as absolute fact.

The continuing change is called progress, with each new truth transforming the previous truth into falsehood. Progress is ineluctable; theories and hypotheses break off like icebergs from a glacier, float off into human knowledge, melt away into history. I wonder why we don't talk much about a certain implication of this eternal process: if the new inevitably overturns the old, then much of what we embrace today is false. It is a liability, this casting of faith with the wrong notion; yet the mind cannot escape it in its groping search for truth.

Whatever the reason, we don't pay much mind to the treacherous nature of knowledge. Which is too bad for eager and innocent young scientists like Richard Bray, romping off to participate in the endless revolutions. You would think the young ones could use a break at this tender juncture in their maturation. You would think that science would value the fresh new viewpoints that young minds are beaming on the mysteries of life.

But such is not the case. Instead, the opposite is true. A young Bray has to try harder. The truth lands on his head, practically shocks the hair out of his follicles. He has the remarkable presence of mind to photograph the event, and it is not enough. He has to make the truth photograph itself. He has to force his way into the society of science, demonstrate his stuff.

Let us return to the big picture and the enormous value to science of angst, irritation, anger, spite, vengeance, spleen, piss 'n' vinegar.

These motives and emotions may seem deplorable, but they make superb sense when you look at science as a product of human nature. What emerges from the haze is a two-tiered system in which scientists find things out and explain them, then take their findings and explanations to their peers for approval.

The first part is the actual science. Something strikes you as odd, interesting. You think, you ponder, you go to bed at night and wake up in the morning trying to understand, to explain. Then inspiration strikes and you *do* understand . . . you think. Now you must devise an experiment that will support or reject your explanation. More cogitation, ponderation, mental absorption. You live for this: it is freedom from the ordinary world, escape from the trials of human interaction, a realm of your own making where the mind lives by its own tastes and desires and terms.

Then you enter the second stage of science, the stage that operates on the official pages of journals; at hiring seminars, symposia, and congresses; at private dinners and parties; during walks and sailing trips; after tennis matches, ski runs, and 10-k races; in laboratories and lavatories—the social stage, where ideas are judged and accepted or rejected by peers.

This is where skepticism comes in. Skepticism is a psychological device that helps a person compete in the game of life. Don't let your rival get anything past you; make sure that what he claims is true. The aim of skepticism is to destroy whatever is false, to pierce, pith, crush, bash, hack, shake, stomp, grind; to analyze, osterize, sterilize, trivialize, pulverize. Under the relentless assault of scientific society, a weak idea will wilt. A false one will disintegrate.

Richard Bray can laugh about his brush with the system. He can laugh because he has succeeded in the game of science and has won a good reputation. He has that reputation in part because of his first, brilliant experiment with an electric fish and a flashbulb. And he performed that elegant piece of science because a skeptical peer refused to accept adequate evidence as proof.

When all is said and done, it is hard to imagine a more efficient device for straining truth from misconception, from bias, illusion, delusion, from the standard errors of the human mind. It is hard to imagine a better motivator than the urge to catch your rival in a fallacy or, better yet, a lie. Spite and vengeance—those emotions can prod inspired contributions from a scientist, as can angst, fear, spleen, and so forth.

Science is the triumph of reason, someone has said, and the world does not argue with such a sweet quote. Looking out in panoramic view over the process of science, however, I am inclined to think that science is not so much the triumph of reason as it is triumph *despite* reason.

DISTRACTING
THE
SNAKE

It's pretty much agreed in this educated society of ours that divorce is one of the great ills of the age. In California, the quoted figure is 50 percent. Fifty percent of all people yoked together this year will resolve their relationship in divorce, and no one seems to know why.

I know why. The reason was revealed to me by my college roommate and a snake of his acquaintance. But this revelation is part of a bigger picture—of relationships and existence and the laws of evolution. That, too, my roommate and the snake revealed.

There is nothing profound about this insight. Nor will it change the status quo. It's not the kind of revelation that people can put to work by rational choice. It merely lets us watch while we writhe on the hook of life, as my roommate used to put it.

This roommate, let us call him Farley, had moved in with me at midsemester of our junior year. I needed someone to help provide the rent, and he wanted more space than the dormitories provided, and fewer regulations. The lack of regulations appealed to Farley, not because he wanted to live the wild life, for he did not: Farley was a strict Mormon devoted to family values; the closest I ever saw him get to a sin was when, during finals, he drank a cup of coffee, and that was only after I had sworn never, ever, to tell his girlfriend of four years' standing. No, Farley was not out for college fun. My apartment appealed to Farley simply because he wanted to have his collection of reptiles under the same roof with him.

Farley loved reptiles, which he called "my herps"—zoological slang derived from "herpetology," the study of reptiles. He often murmured this as a term of endearment to his lizards and snakes while rocking them in one hand and stroking them with the other. His blue eyes would beam with pleasure and little lines of humor and kindness would crinkle up at the corners.

Farley was one of those wiry types blessed, or cursed, with phenomenal energy, and it expressed itself in everything he did. He never just ambled here and there; he leaped, he darted. Farley never slid a chair back to stand up; he rammed it back. He would be sitting there in the next room engrossed in his zoology text, and suddenly a great agonized yawp would issue from the linoleum and you'd hear his feet gallop over to the refrigerator. The refrigerator door would open and slam and he would say in an odd, nasal singsong, "We'll have to go shopping. The herps need food." His voice rose to the highest pitch on the word "need," then dropped abruptly to the lowest note on "food," in a rhythm reminiscent of W. C. Fields.

Well, Farley and his herps moved into my one-bedroom apartment, where the only place to put the assortment of snakes and lizards was in the bedroom on the desks and bookshelves. He had five aquariums in all, stocked with creatures that made a man think before drifting off to sleep. Two humans and ten or so reptiles, all sharing the same room.

There were five or six desert iguanas (*Dipsosaurus dorsalis*), gentle lizards with black and white spots on a light gray background;

they loved nothing so much as basking all day under the heat lamps. There was the four-foot kingsnake (*Lampropeltis getulus*) with its yellow rings spaced at half-inch intervals along the brown-black luster of its scaled skin. Next door to the snake lived a leopard lizard (*Crotaphytus wislizeni*), with jaws like a tiny *Tyrannosaurus*. Its favorite trick was to wait until you leaned down to get a closer look, then it would snap its mouth open and gape. Teeth curved in crescent rows around the upper and lower jaws, all the more striking because the mouth was black. The leopard lizard ate other lizards, which it swallowed headfirst, stuffing the entire animal down into the chamber of molecular disassembly.

This lizard was not a comfort to me, I have to admit. Reptiles in general, and snakes in particular, have always made my skin crawl. This was not to say I cannot appreciate their beauty and their contribution to the big blue world, for I can. But I cannot rid myself of this visceral reaction. In fact, one of the reasons I accepted his menagerie was the chance to learn reptile tolerance, even, I hoped, fondness. One could not ask a better tutor, for Farley was completely without fear of reptiles.

Just to illustrate the point, the first time I witnessed the gaping threat of the leopard lizard I blurted out the obvious: "My God! I bet that thing can really bite!" To which Farley replied in a casual, off-hand way: "Oh, I don't know—it's not that bad."

To this I had no choice but to utter that ancient, reflexive challenge: "Oh yeah? Well, let's see you stick your finger in its mouth."

Without the slightest hesitation, Farley lifted the aquarium lid and reached in with his right hand. The *Crotaphytus* tensed, its black mouth gaped. Farley's hand moved directly toward it. At the instant Farley's index finger got within range, the lizard leaped and clamped. Then, as if concentrating its energy, it closed its eyes, pulled its forelegs up under its armpits, and transferred its entire, lizard-eating soul into its mouth. You could see the jaw muscles straining under the skin.

Farley didn't flinch. He calmly lifted his hand from the cage with the creature hanging on, dangling four feet above the floor. After about thirty seconds, the point having been made, Farley lowered the pet back into its cage. But it refused to let go. Farley took hold of its body and pulled; the lizard clamped down harder, resolve rippling through the bunched muscles of its jaws. Farley pulled harder still; the creature's eyelids squeezed tighter. Its eyeballs sank into its head with the effort. Finally, after several minutes of futile manipulations, Farley said, "Okay, get a spoon."

This I did, and with his free hand my new roommate worked the handle between the lizard's lips and pried its jaws from his finger. He was bleeding. Several teeth had broken off in his flesh. But this bothered him not in the slightest. A Band-Aid and some antibacterial unguent, and Farley was none the worse for the experience.

Another time we went snake-hunting in the mountains behind the university. In the late afternoon the snakes would crawl onto the roads and bask in the heat which the tarmac had absorbed. A collector of herps had only to drive down the road with open eyes, and the groggy, heat-besotted reptiles were his for the taking.

We were driving along in Farley's rusted VW bug, the sunroof open and Farley's head sticking out the top. He had worked out a way of sitting on a rolled sleeping bag so that he was almost standing but was still able to reach the foot pedals. With his head above the roof he could scan 360 degrees around and watch the road as well as the roadsides and the adjacent fields.

Down the road we went, breathing the warm spring air laden with the scent of chaparral. Suddenly Farley slammed on the brakes and we skidded in a shower of gravel and dust onto the shoulder of the road. Before we even came to a stop, he flung open the door, dashed across the road, dived between the strands of a barbed wire fence, ducked into a forward roll as he hit the ground. He came up running, dived again, slid along on his stomach while reaching straight ahead with his right arm, and grabbed something as he slid to a stop, something that looked like a rope.

"Bring the pick!" he yelled. "Bring the pick and the sack!"

I came running with the tools (after climbing very carefully between the barbed wires), and I saw that Farley was holding the tail of a snake. It was all he had managed to grasp before it disappeared down a gopher hole. Judging from the markings it was in fact a gopher snake (*Pituophis catenifer*), a nonvenomous species that nonetheless was often willing to bite.

Snatching the geologist's pick, Farley hacked away at the soil, tossing clods and debris into the air. With a cry of triumph, he ripped up one last clod and wrenched the snake from the earth. Whereupon it whipped around and fastened its jaws onto Farley's wrist. Blood streamed from the wound. But my roommate calmly, gently grasped the reptile with both hands and began stroking and manipulating its straining body; no matter where the reptile pointed its head, one of Farley's hands was always there to cradle it, guide it back toward Farley's midriff. After a few minutes the creature, which had been so desperate, was limp and docile. I held the sack open, and Farley slipped the snake in.

"My God, Farley," I said, eyeing the blood, "doesn't that hurt? Doesn't that bother you?"

"No," said my unperturbed friend. "I don't mind it when they bite. What bothers me is when they go on you."

I knew then we could never be close. Our values were too different. I would gladly endure soilage with a dollop from the bowels of a snake, I would endure a multiple deposit, but please, please, dear Maker, spare me from its teeth!

Not all of Farley's pets were so militant. My favorite was a whiptail lizard, *Cnemidophorus tigris*, and it was actually rather sweet. It had a long, slender tail that whipped about when it ran, and its eyelids had probably the slowest, sleepiest stroke in the vertebrate kingdom. I remember wondering if they ever got stuck halfway across the eye for lack of ambition. The eyelids were doubly disconcerting because they were transparent; they played tricks with your mind the first time you saw them blink. "What the . . . ," you'd think. "I could swear that animal just closed its eyes. *But it's still staring at me!*"

Its friendly disposition, though, was its most endearing trait. It would sit for hours on Farley's shoulder while he studied. Sometimes, when the urge came on, it would walk down Farley's arm to the desk, where he kept an ashtray of water. Standing before it like a little dog, the *Cnemidophorus* would bend down and lap the fluid with a long, forked tongue. Satisfied, it would turn deliberately around, walk back up Farley's arm to the shoulder, and resume its observations.

Then there was the star of Farley's collection, his prize possession, *Heloderma suspectum*, the gila monster.

Now, this was one specimen that truly spooked me. For one thing, the gila monster possesses a neurotoxic venom, and I didn't care for that one bit, as neurotoxins tend to paralyze your breathing equipment. But what bothered me most was its looks. The creature just looked evil. It was a thick, lumpy thing at least two feet long, with a massive, hugely muscled head. It was covered with a dusty black skin whose scales looked like Indian beads, and like Indian beads, some were orange and arranged randomly in blotches over the body. All day long it would lie in its cave, a cardboard box. When it did move it ambled with slow, clumsy jerks like a robot. That was deceptive, though, because it was capable, when aroused, of lunging and clamping its jaws with invisible speed. If it got a solid bite (which I never saw it do) it was said to grind away, the venom running down grooves on the rear edges of its teeth into the victim's flesh. Farley would feed it eggs, which it crushed and then lapped slowly, mechanically, like a machine. I am happy to report that we never had any trouble with Farley's prize pet; it just endured in its box while we endured the travails of education, and eventually I grew used to its malevolent presence.

Life went on routinely once we got used to each other's eccentricities. Up at 7:00, study for an hour or so, off to classes, back for dinner, study and write reports until 12:00 or 1:00, to bed—and on and on, week after week. Midterm exams and laboratory practicals came and went in mind-numbing waves. But there was one event that everyone looked forward to without exception: the three-day field trip to the high desert.

This was the climax of field zoology, one of the few courses in modern biology where students actually go out into nature and convene with wild things. It was taught by a professor whom I shall call Marlowe, a man who enjoyed the rare good fortune of making a living by studying what he had always loved, which was wildlife. Our mission would be to observe reptiles in their natural environment, then collect and take them back to the university so the professors could further their research careers.

We launched the expedition on a Friday morning, twenty students wedged into three university Land Rovers, caravaning up from the San Bernardino Valley through the Cajon Pass toward Victorville in the Mojave Desert. Reaching Cajon Summit, we stopped and gazed. To creatures like us, living our existence in such artificial oases as the Southern California valleys, what we saw was completely alien. It could have been the surface of Mars. We climbed back into our automotive capsules and rolled into the desert, blank eyes shielded by black glasses, vacant minds stunned by the truths laid bare and harsh on the soil itself.

Our eyes ran along the edges of jagged, naked mountains; they stumbled down steep gullies, bounced off boulders, snagged on sharp outcrops, skidded to a stop on the rough sand of the desert floor. Then the plants—our eyes raced over the plants, punctured themselves on the bristling thorns of cholla cactus, impaled themselves on the flesh-piercing blades of the Spanish bayonet and the Joshua tree, and groped in vain for shelter beneath the spindly, greasy creosote bush, shelter from the nuclear force of the sun.

Energy raged around us. Light glared, reflected. Heat shimmered, burned, penetrated. We had entered the realm of desiccation. Here the hot, dry air pulled the moisture from everything but sealed containers. The mountains to the west saw to that; they blocked the clouds that came wallowing inland from the sea, lugging water in their fat gray bellies; as the price of passage the mountains demanded the entire freight. As a result, the few clouds that survived the passage had nothing left to drop on this arid world of sand. That was why this land met the official criterion for desert: the evaporation rate was more than twice the rate of precipitation. We could feel the air sucking the moisture from our lips. Our eyes felt hot. We were inside air-conditioned vehicles, yet still we could feel the desert's force.

But what of the animals and plants out on that interphase, where each day the sun sears the earth's naked skin with a torrent of photons? How did life survive the blasting of the sun?

Life survived by twisting and wringing the molecules of DNA: by altering leaves, bark, roots, even the metabolic chemistry; by recasting body, color, skin, eyes, ears, nose. Over the eons all things inhabiting this zone of burning matter had had to meet the strictest of biological building codes. This was a lesson Professor Marlowe had brought us here to learn.

We gazed at the plants—the wonderful, grotesque plants scattered here and there in the sand, and we pondered them as we sped to our tryst with the reptiles. Plant and animal. Both designed and built to resist the heat, to seal the precious water in their cells, to live in a kind of harsh yet mutual relationship—the plant armored with thorns and spines, the reptile armored with chitinous scales and plates so that it might crawl invulnerably over the botanical blades. It was the kind of relationship that the biologist learns, finally, to accept as the truth of life.

Each living thing had been crafted for existence in this searing land. The plants were particularly modified, since they had no way of avoiding the sun and the heat once they put down roots. To conserve water, evolution had rolled the leaves of some into thorns; it had coated the leaves of others, like the creosote bush, with oil and finished the skin of the cacti and the yuccas with wax. To reflect light and deflect heat and to shield the surface from the sucking wind, evolution had clothed the the foliage of the burro bush, the salt bushes, and many other species with a pelt of short, dense hairs that imparted a gray coloration.

Even the most fundamental of plant processes, photosynthesis, had been modified to husband water. Most plants perform this task during the day; they open the pores known as stomata to take in carbon dioxide, then feed it directly into the photosynthetic machinery, which creates carbohydrates. But the plants on which we gazed could not afford to open their pores during the day, for that would be suicidal: that would release precious water. So these desert plants had hit upon an ingenious metabolic solution: they performed the crucial task of taking in carbon dioxide during the night, after the air, which cannot hold as much moisture when cool, loses much of its desiccating power. But because the desert plants did the job at night, they needed a way to store the carbon dioxide for use during the day. And here was where the ingenuity struck. The desert plants converted the gas to mallic acid, a liquid. The following day they could convert the acid back to carbon dioxide and proceed with photosynthesis under the sun, as all plants must.

We camped that night near the Amboy Crater, a black, chunky infant of a volcano swaddled in white dunes. The next morning we arose slowly. In the high desert spring, reptiles don't start moving until the sun has warmed the sand. Since many species bury themselves in the sand at night, they wait until the sand warms, which in turn warms their torpid bodies. Since there was none of the traditional need to arise at the glimmer of dawn—the reptiles wouldn't be up and about for several hours at least—we luxuriated in a leisurely breakfast around the cookfire. We washed and combed and broke camp. Then we girded for the hunt.

Each of us was issued a large, dirty cotton sack to hold the reptiles and a "lizard stick" to catch them with. The lizard stick was a slender six-foot bamboo rod fitted at the tip with an adjustable noose of monofilament fishing line. The idea was to sneak up behind a lizard or snake and, very slowly, very gently, maneuver the noose over its head and lift, which created a dangling herp, its entire world wrenched away.

Professor Marlowe gave us final instructions: Fan out from the camp, collect whatever you can get, watch out for sidewinders and other rattlesnakes under the bushes, and regroup here at noon. Then he released us into the desert.

We trudged off through the soft white sand, our footprints filling in with each step. Our eyes coursed and darted over the surroundings, picked through the spines and thorns and oily, waxy vegetation; they probed in particular beneath the creosote bushes, where the sidewinders were supposed to bury themselves.

Now and then we would actually see a lizard, but not often. Their markings blended superbly with the thin, dappled shade under the desert shrubs, and before you could decipher their form, they scooted away to safety. "Scoot" is not urgent enough. The zebra-tailed lizard (*Callisaurus draconoides*), for instance, rose up on its hind legs as it gained speed and dashed off like a little human sprinter, except for the tail, which it curled forward over its head. We could not run twenty miles per hour as they could, so we let them get away. Another species, the fringe-toed lizard (*Uma scoparia*), had the disturbing habit of lying buried in the sand, and just as you were passing one it would burst from the earth and careen off over the dunes at twenty-three miles per hour. With each demonstration, the superb adaptation of these creatures became more clear.

Like the desert plants, these desert reptiles had been crafted by their relationship to dryness, grit, and spines. They could, for example, climb with impunity among the needles of even so treacherous a plant as the cholla, the leaping cactus. This plant is so densely clothed in spines that in the early morning or late afternoon, when the sun is low, the needles glow in the backlight, encasing the plant in a fur of light. Here and there stood these photosynthesizing priests, leading the assembled crowds of desert shrubs in a celebration of light.

In their own way, the reptiles were just as glorious. The fringe-toed lizard, for instance, was designed for life *in* the sand. When one would burst from beneath the surface and sprint away, it would run twenty or thirty yards, stop abruptly, turn at right angles to its route, and disappear again beneath the surface—all in no more than a few seconds. They are also fitted out with the right tools and with the right behavior to operate the tools. Their upper jaw overlaps the bottom, which keeps sand from entering the mouth when digging. Their nasal passages loop down into a chamber which traps sand and prevents it from entering the lungs. Flaps of skin seal off the ears and nostrils when the animal burrows. Their toes are ingeniously modified, equipped with fringes for extra traction on and under a granular surface. Even their eyes are specialized for life in the sand: The fringes of the upper and lower eyelids project into fingers which interdigitate when the eyelids close; no grain of sand can wedge them apart. If sand enters the open eye, a third eyelid, known as the nictitating membrane, pushes the grains from the corner out. The nictitating membrane is also transparent (like the eyelid of Farley's *Cnemidophorus*); these desert lizards can therefore sit in the wind, watching imperviously as the stinging grains whistle by.

These details swirled in our minds as we walked along that morning, in intellectual harmony with the physical setting: the notions of evolution; the sensual slope and structure of the dunes; the ecology of plants; the beauty of gray foliage and the miracle of needles and spines; the ethology of lizards; the ingenuity of scale, eyelid, and nasal sand trap. We stood there on the sand, motes on the flat vastness, and felt the silence. The silence increased, became a pressure. The pressure in turn became sound again, the thumping of life, the rush of fluid through arteries, arterioles, veins, the flow of life in the nation of cells that a creature is, and this creature stood now in the alien yet familiar dryness.

For the first time we saw also that evolution puts limits on us all.

For each ability gained, there is an ability lost. These plants and creatures of the desert had been crafted for life under sun, on sand, in heat, in arid air. Like fish in water, they had no meaning, nor could they survive, anywhere else. Life exists on the stage where its role is writ, and this holds true for all of evolution's creatures.

We did, in the end, manage to capture some of those creatures. At noon we reassembled at the campsite and began a show-and-tell on the college level. Taking turns, we explained what we had caught and how we had caught them, and then we removed our catch. We laid our sacks on the ground and gingerly groped through the cloth until we located a creature; pinning it down, we worked the other hand down into the sack; then, with a firm grip, we very carefully pulled the animal from the bag.

This went on until a fellow named Barry, the president of the local fraternity, came walking in with a sack bulging with large, writhing lumps.

"What've you got there?" asked Doctor Marlowe.

"A gopher snake," said Barry, "it's got to be six feet."

"Take it out. Let's see it."

"Uh—I don't think we should, Doctor Marlowe. I think it's a biter."

"Hmmm."

Not even the professor was keen to handle such a creature. Big gopher snakes will strike instinctively at the face, and at six feet in length, even a nonpoisonous snake could open some nasty wounds. We gathered around to stare at the thing in the sack. No one knew what to do.

"What's going on here?" came a voice lilting across the sand, and Farley walked briskly into camp holding his own sack of reptiles.

"Barry's got a six-foot gopher snake, and it's mad," someone said. "Nobody wants to take it out."

"All right, everyone. Stand back." Farley pushed his way through the crowd. "*I'll* take care of this."

He grabbed the sack. In one swipe of the hand he untied the

drawstring and jerked the sack open. A great communal hiss soared into the desert sky as the whole group, realizing what Farley was about to do, sucked in horrified air. Without so much as a glance inside, he plunged his arm into the sack, up to his armpit. The sack thrashed, the snake hissed, the arm wrestled. Farley stood up straight. Holding the sack with his left hand, he pulled forth his right arm and, with a magician's flourish, presented the snake.

It was even larger than we had thought, probably seven or eight feet of muscle, tendon, cartilage, skin, bone, and large, sharp teeth. It was a desert gopher snake, *Pituophis catenifer*, subspecies *deserticola*, with regular black patches against a cream-colored background. It had wound itself in overlapping coils up and down Farley's arm, from the base of his thumb to the middle of his biceps; coils as thick as a rolling pin were wound tight and flexing, ending in a head the size of a medium avocado. The head snaked this way and that, sizing up its predicament with orange-red eyes and black dilated pupils. There seemed to be an intelligence behind those eyes, a mind glinting at the crowd.

The coils contracted and expanded continuously, some seeming to move up the arm, others downward. For an existential instant, Farley's arm became the arm of Medusa, the flesh of human and serpent unified into a single massive, crawling and contracting organ. But only for an instant. Then the lesson in relationships began.

Being a snake, the creature had no choice but to play out the programs wired into its nature. So, wrapped securely around Farley's arm, it lunged hissing at the faces of Farley's peers. We leaped back, sucking air. The snake rewound itself and cocked its neck for another strike. We moved in for another look. Again the snake hissed and struck; again we shrank back, pulling air in a great, choral inspiration, recoiling from the snake in our evolutionary past. Back and forth lunged the snake and the students; in and out went the air, in and out of terrified creatures. Again and again the theater of instinct repeated itself.

Meanwhile, as the ageless play was acted out, Farley worked quietly, methodically, with the snake. It strained continuously to move forward, an action it could not restrain under these circumstances. And wherever it turned to move, it always found Farley's hand supporting its neck, providing substance over which to move. Both his arms were moving in a slow, circular motion, left synchronized with right so that while one hand was supporting the snake near Farley's stomach, the other was reaching out to support and direct the head. Gradually the animal grew calmer. Finally, after about five minutes, it came to a complete rest. Just a great lump of serpentine rope looped over Farley's arm. Then Farley offered to pass the creature around; according to this master of snakes, the monster would permit it. The first student held out her hands, her eyes snapping shut when the cool coils touched her skin, snapping back open in blank amazement when she realized that indeed the creature was compliant; several minutes later, driven by demands to share, she passed the creature on.

And that was how the scene ended, twenty students of the desert stroking an enormous old master of the white sand and creosote bush.

Farley and I got back to the apartment late that night. Gear had to be sorted and stored away. Lizards and snakes from the desert had to be placed in their new apartments, introduced to their new roommates. But things had changed between Farley and me, and as we worked I looked at him with new respect.

"Farley," I said, four *Crotophytuses* glaring up at us, black mouths gaping malice. "You were magnificent out there—a real hero. But tell me. How do you *do* it? What's the secret to handling snakes?"

"Oh, it's simple," said my roommate. Then he said a curious thing: "It's just like a relationship. The secret to handling snakes, or any wild animal for that matter, is to always keep it pointed at someone else. That way it takes you for granted and takes out its anger on the other guy. You're like the ground, the dirt it stands on. The outside world is the threat."

He looked at me shrewdly. He knew I'd try to find the exception to the rule.

"What if there's no one else around?"

"Then it'll probably turn around and bite you."

We return now to the topic of divorce, for there it was, the truth revealed. The reasoning was simple and direct, and it cleaved the convolutions of the social sciences down to the biological bone. It could be stated thus in a simple evolutionary axiom: Use it or lose it. It is an axiom, however, that requires some background in the theory of ecology and evolution.

If you have acquired a *thing* in the course of your evolutionary alterations, then you must use that thing. A thing can be any thing. It can be a wing, an eye, a leg. Birds that live on islands tend to lose the power of flight; fish, crickets, and other creatures that have spent evolutionary time in caves lose their eyes; snakes and certain lizards that travel directly on the ground have lost their legs. In the big scheme of things, existence is the most difficult of all victories, and there is no place for extra baggage. It takes away from the task at hand.

An unused thing is usually a liability. For a bird that does not need to fly, wings are clumsy devices that must be carried for no purpose. For cave creatures, eyes are useless mechanisms constructed at the cost of genetic information and molecular labor—a cost better spent on other senses in a cave. For snakes and certain burrowing lizards, legs, besides the genetic cost of creation, require nerves, muscle, and brain space to operate; they also snag on rocks and drag against the sand and soil during emergencies. No, you do not want any device that does not help you survive.

How is a part lost? If it is a liability, then it will select against itself. Creatures slowed by a useless leg, say, will tend to die sooner, leaving fewer genes behind. It is a painful truth, but pain never gave evolution any reason for pause.

This brings us back to human relationships and marriage. The ability to have a relationship is an evolved thing. The ability takes genetic space and brain space. The wisdom of popular psychology holds that people *learn* how to relate, *learn* their social skills—and they do. But they are *able* to learn because their brain is *constructed* to learn those particular tasks. People overlook the fundamental significance of that fact, but you cannot form a human relationship with a nonhuman thing (and I say that in complete bondage to a cat). Each species is designed and built to form its own relationships, its own social skills, even if the relationship lasts no longer than the act of copulation.

So what are relationships for? What is their purpose? How do they fit into the big, evolutionary scheme of life?

Relationships *must* be for the survival of genes. What else? That is the purpose of life, to survive long enough to pass the genetic wand to the next generation. Human males and human females form teams for the struggle. It's as basic as that.

I doubt that any of us can comprehend how brutal the fight for survival has been throughout evolution. We ignore our legacy, a world in which most children died in infancy or childhood, where teeth rotted out by the age of twenty, where gangrene took the lives of the injured, where thirty-five was foul old age. Even as recently as 1750 in London, the toll of disease staggers the mind: Of 2,239 children born in that year, only 168 were still alive five years later. The Weekly Bill of Mortality for August 15–22, 1665, shows people dying of such ills as "Riting of the Lights—18"; "Stone—2"; "Teeth—111"; "Winde—4"; "Wormes—20"; "Griping in the Guts—79"; "Suddenly—2"; "Stopping of the Stomach—17"; "Grief—3"; "Childbed—28"; "Convulsion—89"; "Frighted—2"; "Feaver—348"; and, of course, the great reaper, "Plague—4,237."

Clearly, life was not meant to be easy. There was no time to worry about the refinements of relating, no time—or very little—to deal with insults, incompatibility, spiritual malaise. The point is, the human brain is designed and engineered to deal with ruthless hardship: it is one rugged piece of work.

It is also the most successful device ever created for easing the burden of life. We of the Western world have drastically reduced the incidence of disease. We have completely conquered our nonhuman predators. Through the use of fossilized energy we have helped to make labor into play, starvation into the rantings of moralists, the cold of winter and the heat of summer into unacceptable hardships. As a result, we have managed to convince ourselves in the last few hundred years that the purpose of life is the pursuit of happiness; since the Second World War we of the West, particularly we Americans, have gone even farther and transformed the pursuit of happiness into the pursuit of outright hedonistic pleasure. This is the great illusion of the twentieth century.

What we have done, in fact, is create a completely alien world. And that plays directly into another axiom of evolution: You have to live where you were made to live. The whale must live in the sea, the swallow in the sky, the flea on another creature. The human being cannot live in the absence of hardship. In fundamental terms, we are not designed for the world we have created. We have the ability to bond in pairs, which in turn have the ability to countervail the dangers, the pains, and the agonies of our ancestral state; but the ability is not being used, *really* used.

What can be done? Probably not much. We cannot alter relationships through sheer will; human nature will not change. Therefore conditions must. Maybe, with the problem defined, we can find a way to simulate the agonies and the ecstasies of traditional survival, but that remains to be seen.

I know only what my roommate and a very large, very angry reptile revealed among the thorns and spines and sands of reality. We are handling a snake. It is watching for threats from the outside world, threats it has evolved to face; to cope is its reason for being. It peers and writhes and strains. Finally, finding nothing to strike, it twists to attack its handler. The snake has nowhere else to turn.

MAKING A
DINOSAUR
WORK

It's hard to make a dinosaur work. For one thing, the eyes sometimes roll before the lids close, which makes for a weird-looking wink. For another, the levers and pistons tend to wear at different rates, and the legs and body can get out of sync. This makes for spasms. In damp climates the skin can get gummy and tacky and stick together, and that's if cracks don't appear in the creases where the skin flexes. The air hoses can leak. The electronics can short out. And always there are those quiet but nagging little puffs and wheezes and clicks and knocks as the air valves open and close, the pistons squeeze in and out, and the eyes flick back and forth. It is not easy to make a dinosaur work, not easy at all.

But then, it's a lot harder to make a dinosaur in the first place, and that is what this story is about—a unique company called Dinamation International, which manufactures robotic dinosaurs and sends them in traveling displays to museums around the world. It's a story about a process of creation in which scientists, engineers, and artists cooperate, and about the philosophic ironies that dinosaurs and robots lay open for contemplation. For "dinamations," to stretch the use of the company name, are monuments to technology, and dinosaurs are monuments to extinction, which brings technology and extinction face to face. But I get ahead of myself; we shall return to that later.

The story of Dinamation International begins with its founder and president, Chris Mays, who in 1982 decided to find a new career. Forty-seven years old, with three grown sons, he had piloted commercial airliners for twenty years. The friendly skies had become boring. His whole life and education had been flying; he had joined the navy at eighteen and flown fighter jets for ten years before joining TWA. But he had the confidence to start over in life (landing on and taking off from aircraft carriers gave him that), and, being one of fourteen brothers and sisters, he had the ability to deal with people. Above all, he had a voracious appetite for learning. Whatever it was he was going to do, he was going to jump in.

Enter Japanese dinosaurs. Mays had seen robotized dinosaurs on public display in Japan. He had also learned that some of them were for sale, having served their purpose in various festivals. There was something intriguing about the opportunity, and he mentioned the matter to a neighborhood acquaintance named Tom Stifter, who had experience in business and marketing. Why not import them for resale? suggested Stifter.

It seemed like a good idea—or at least half of one. The other half was where to sell them. Museums seemed the logical choice, but in the early eighties, funding was being cut and no one could afford to buy dinamations. Besides that, there was no evidence that people would accept mechanical dinosaurs.

Then came one of those serendipitous events that appear to be guided by fate, and the doubts vanished. The Los Angeles County Museum of Natural History was having a patrons' banquet, and Mays offered to donate a half-sized triceratops to provide ambience for the evening. Set up in the dining hall, it mesmerized the patrons. The idea of joint-venture exhibits quickly evolved, and Dinamation was in the business of sending displays to museums in return for part of the proceeds.

The exhibits have been a sensation. Attendance usually multiplies three to fifteen times, and it is not unusual for a museum to attract as many visitors in one to three months as it would see in an entire year.

The dinosaurs, however, have improved dramatically in contrast to the original Japanese prototypes. Their appearance is far truer to the scientific facts, and they are far more sophisticated in their mechanics. Nor is the company restricting itself to dinosaurs. With eternity as its territory, Dinamation intends to romp through the eons at will and to date has manufactured robotic versions of woolly mammoths, saber-toothed cats, and giant ground sloths, as well as a series of future animals based on the (optimistic) assumption that evolution is going to go on for a few more years yet. Prehistoric whales, sharks, and plesiosaurs are in the works, and there are plans for exhibits on giant insects, endangered species, and earthquake mechanics (this to be a hands-on display allowing one to see what happens along a geological fault, say, when a control lever alters one subterranean stress or another).

All this reflects the fact that Dinamation is more than a corporation dedicated to making a profit. It is a company dedicated to education—science education in particular.

"Why not give something back?" says Mays. "I saw Dinamation as fulfilling some pent-up frustrations I had about people who have become the heroes of today. Primarily they're created by the media—they're rock stars, they're sports people, they're pampered and drugged-up athletes, and the list goes on and on. Why in the world are those people heroes? What I want to do is turn our scientists and our teachers and our creatures into heroes. Let us make education fun, make it a participatory thing. And we certainly have the hook.

Everything we make at Dinamation has been scrutinized for what it can bring to the public."

So the company has developed an educational master plan whose avowed purpose is to add fun and entertainment to the substance of science. Dinosaurs are the axle around which the master plan rotates. The Dinamation staff have even coined a term for it—"dinoscience"—and feel confident that dinosaurs can be used to teach any aspect of science.

The hands-on display, and in particular the remote-controlled dimetrodon, is one of the most telling devices. The dimetrodons were a group of mammalian ancestors that looked superficially like ten-to-twelve-foot lizards fitted with an enormous dorsal fin, similar in shape to that of the sailfish. In the Dinamation display, however, the skin has been removed, so what one sees is the internal workings of a robot. By cranking a joystick, visitors can make the mouth open and close, the head, legs, and tail move, while the pistons stroke and puff and the rods swing.

This and the hundreds of robotic dinosaurs are the most publicized aspect of Dinamation's mission to educate, but the master plan extends far beyond the museum. The company bankrolls paleontological research; it sponsors dinosaur digs for lay people; it co-produced "Dinosaurs, Dinosaurs—A Mesozoic Musical," which is performed by an actor named Slim Goodbody in museums and other venues; it helped found a dinosaur museum in Grand Junction, Colorado; and it publishes a quarterly journal, *Dinosauria*, devoted to dinosaur paleontology. The proceeds from the dinamations support all of this.

The response to automated dinosaurs eventually grew so strong that Mays and Stifter decided it was time to enter the business of manufacturing their own, and they opened a plant near their homes in Southern California. It couldn't have been located in a more appropriate place than the land of dreams, for Disneyland and Knott's Berry Farm are located minutes up the freeway. But there was to be one fundamental difference between the Dinamation fantasies and the others, and that was the rigor of science. Mickey Mouse, Donald Duck, Goofy, and Bigfoot are creations of pure whimsy; dinamations are the most accurate reconstructions it is possible to make from scientific insight and modern technology. This is where the story becomes truly interesting, because it demands cooperation of scientists, engineers, and artists—not a natural union.

Creation starts with scientists, with the paleontologists who decipher the fossilized archives of the eons. Paleontology is a sort of forensic biology, and it has come of age in the past twenty years. With an ever growing number of high-tech devices and methods, these students of the dead are conjuring up more and more skin and flesh and placing it back onto the bones of ancient creatures. They do not stop with the physical form. How did the creature make its living? What did it eat, what kind of land did it live on, did it care for its young, was it social, did it travel in groups, was it warm-blooded, how did it reproduce? All the information that any biologist would want to know about a living animal is what these forensic biologists are seeking.

The internal structure of the bones suggests that at least some dinosaurs may have been warm-blooded. Stones in the stomach cavity indicate that some pulverized their food not with teeth, but with rock-loaded gizzards. The grooves and scars on the teeth of a predator indicate whether or not it chewed on bones; the bones in turn reveal the kind of teeth that did the chewing. And the fossilized tracks—now, there lies drama! A field of footprints in Texas has recorded a herd of *Apatosaurus* traveling along a river; huge adults, male or female, guarded the perimeter; the calves assembled inside the adult barrier. And skirting the huge herbivores are the tracks of *Allosaurus*, a forty-five-foot predator waiting to strike.

Making a dinamation requires all this information and more, particularly with regard to internal anatomy, and even here it is amazing what the fossils can tell: how much weight the skeleton was designed to support; what kinds of motion the bones could articulate; where the muscles were attached, and how large they were. With years and years in which to contemplate, there is no end to the clever insights the paleontologists are able to generate.

To meet their own stringent standards Dinamation retains a Who's Who of paleontology. The board of advisors lists such luminaries as Bob Bakker, Adjunct Curator of Paleontology at the University of Colorado; Harley J. Armstrong, Curator of Paleontology at the Museum of Western Colorado; and George L. Callison, Professor of Biology at California State University at Long Beach. If they are not enough, the company brings in additional experts. Callison, an expert on small dinosaurs, is also on staff as Dinamation's science advisor and exercises continuous influence as the creatures leave the drawing board, and enter the machine shop, the sculpting studio, and the molding area.

After one to one and a half years of research, a beast is ready to meet its makers—literally. This occurs in a "new creatures meeting," and here the vastly different (I would venture to say, completely opposite) minds meet: scientists and engineers versus artists and sculptors. It is the central interaction in the creation of a technological dinosaur, and it succeeds beyond all expectations.

In abstract theory, if you compare the essence of the artist and the essence of the scientist, the union should not work. In this ideal world the artist would create entirely from within, from the imagination. The scientist would acquire all facts on the issue—the antithesis of imagination. So when the two minds converge in this theoretical scenario, the goal of the scientist is at direct odds with the goal of the artist. Ideally, the scientist would bring the dinosaur itself to the meeting, thereby reducing the artist to the role of mere illustrator.

This doesn't happen, of course. Dinosaurs come in such an incredible range of sizes and shapes and are loaded with so many odd extras (bone-helmet skulls, trombone-crest horns, radiator spinal plates, thumb spikes, one-of-a-kind tooth arrangements) that not even the wildest imagination can outdo reality. And the fact remains that for all their forensic skills and all their technical expertise, the scientists still have just the bones, tracks, eggs, and a few skin impressions to work with. They need the artist's imagination to make a dinosaur.

George Callison explains what goes on in the science/art collaboration: "We talk about tongues and the color of tongues and how the tongues moved. We talk about lips and skin and eye colors and the size of muscle mass, and all kinds of things that scientists never spent much time thinking about before because they're not needed in classifying dinosaurs. It's a whole different thing, trying to create lifelike animals out of rubber skin and fake hair and tubing and metal."

At a new creatures meeting, then, Callison or Bakker or some other advisor leads off with speculative facts about the creature under consideration. The plesiosaur, for instance, that long-necked, snake-headed, four-flippered dragon of the Cretaceous oceans, appears from the bones to have moved its neck only in the horizontal plane. This means it could not have arched its neck vertically the way it has always been depicted, but must have bowed it horizontally instead, like a snake coiling to strike. But it was a long neck, and the chief engineer makes a practical point: How do you get the skin to adhere to the metal without bunching while the creature cocks for the strike?

Another creature under consideration is a strange marine fossil known as *Pterogotus*. It was flat as a wafer, maybe five inches thick, but six feet long; it looked like a scorpion with pincers and jointed legs; and it is thought to have swum like a crab, sculling along with a paddle on either side, using its tail as a rudder. The practical banter goes on endlessly.

"We could cast it in sections," remarks an engineer, "then fit them together so they overlap."

"Yeah," says a sculptor, "but the color should be cast in the material, then, so that it doesn't wear off where the edges rub."

The robotics expert points to the diagram of the tail and asks, "Does this mean it has a range of motion of about sixty degrees?"

"Yes," says one of the scientists.

"How about translation? Is there a sideways translation in the tail, and if so, how much—about five degrees to each side?"

"Yes," says the scientist.

"Well, this might not be as tough as it looks."

The conversation wheels freely for an hour. Black cloth might be suitable for the "skin" that connects the overlapping plates on the creature's back. A colored gel could be painted inside the mold, fusing the color to the urethane foam body. The creature could be mounted on a rock, with the air compressor and the computer for motion control housed inside. Practical talk. The nuts and bolts of creation.

After the new creatures meeting, the project goes to the sculpture and engineering departments. While draftsmen draw blueprints for the internal robotics, artists bring the fossil to life, first in detailed anatomical sketches, then in a small clay maquette. The detail on these miniature statues is exquisite, the wrinkles around the eyes so precise, the wrinkles on the skin so realistic, the expression on the face so convincing that if they began walking around the room you'd just assume they were pets. Little woolly mammoths, triceratops, stegosaurs, tyrannosaurs, diplodocus—they stand on tables, walk across benches, lurk on filing cabinets, each representing a new creature in miniature.

Next a full-size or scale-size statue is sculpted of clay. If the original creature could have fit into a North American Van Lines eighteen-wheeler, Dinamation builds a full-size model—as with *Allosaurus, Deinonychus,* and *Dimetrodon.* If the creature was too large for North American to accommodate, Dinamation scales the model down to a size that will fit. Apatosaurs, stegosaurs, and triceratops have been reduced. *Tyrannosaurus rex*, however, has been decapitated in the drawing room and only the head constructed; its full-sized head is more impressive than a complete animal scaled down.

A skin of urethane foam is then molded in sections from this clay statue. The "plates" are body panels made of fiberglass or some other rigid, lightweight material. When assembled, they form the "plucked chicken"—the creature's body—over which the skin will be laid.

Meanwhile, as the body is being built, the engineers are busy designing robots that will fit inside the dinamation and drive the moving parts. The robots in turn are driven by compressed air, and all the pistons, levers, air tubes, and electrical wiring must be in place, functioning, and finely tuned before the skin and the model are "married." A Dinamation marriage takes at least a day and includes such tedious but crucial tasks as getting the eye holes to fit precisely over the eyeballs and padding out any saggy areas of the skin.

Then comes the matter of programming the creature's actions, including grunts, groans, roars, mewlings—whatever *Homo sapiens* can rationalize, for fossils are mute and give no guidelines. Sounds allow almost complete license, and the sound programmer has the unfettered choice of any recorded natural sound. The snarls, roars, coughs, yowls, growls, mewls, grunts, etc., of tigers, anteaters, bears, hippopotamus, elephants, etc., are grist for his mill, or, rather, his digital synthesizer, which translates the sounds into good, colloquial Dinosaur.

For actions and behavior, the programmer borrows from living animals, because if you imitate the familiar, you at least get the illusion of life. It may be entirely false, but it rings true.

A typical loop program runs three or four minutes, which is long enough to give the impression of a continually emerging drama. It is true choreography, too, a little scene that science advisor Callison scripts with dramatic structure. It usually begins in domestic tranquility—a triceratops, say, browsing quietly. Suddenly it senses something. Its head jerks up. It sniffs the air. Its eyes flick back and forth. It steps menacingly forward. It throws back its head and roars. (Little children watching this cling to their daddy's legs; some burst into tears; others laugh hysterically.) Then, with its foe sufficiently intimidated and the drama resolved, the dinosaur returns to its blissful browsing.

Human feedback has sprung a few surprises. In the beginning, Dinamation presumed that the more spectacular the movement, the better people would like it. In actual fact, the big, sweeping arc of a brontosaur's neck proved less compelling than the subtle jerk of a triceratops's head. The most intriguing observation, though, was the human response to eye movement. The eyes have turned out to be the most important of all the moving parts: They are organs which have "high information content," revealing the owner's emotions and intentions, and like all creatures, *Homo sapiens* instinctively seeks them out. So Dinamation has learned what actors have always known—that subtle movements of intention can be more powerful than broad sweeps of the body and limbs. (Smaller movements also have the fortuitous benefit of being easier on the skin, since the urethane eventually fatigues along the lines of flexion.)

Once the program is composed and installed, the dinamation is turned on and allowed to run for forty hours or so to reveal any program glitches and weak points in the skin. The robot has to be tuned. Thirty or forty valves have to be adjusted so that air is piped at just the right instant to the pistons that move the legs, eyes, mouth, and other parts. Air is compressible, and because it must journey through tubes of differing lengths, there is a certain amount of "slop" that cannot be avoided in these pneumatic systems.

Eventually the creature is ready for the final touch: painting. It is lifted onto a stake-bed truck and hauled across town to Dinamation's painting facility. There a crew of artists apply the stripes and patterns and colors that seem plausible in light of living birds and mammals. Again, the illusion of reality is the goal.

When the paint is dry, the new creation is anointed and sent on its maiden voyage—back across town to the Dinamation factory. Words cannot describe the effect a full-grown *Allosaurus* has on the motorists of Southern California as it rides along in a flatbed truck, mouth agape.

It is late afternoon, and the Dinamation factory is largely deserted. Dinosaurs crowd the factory floor. A half-assembled *Allosaurus* stands before you, cable hanging from its eye socket like the optic nerve it is, the leg skins pulled loosely up over the calves and open at the top like rubber waders. Next to it sits a gigantic, life-sized bust of *Tyrannosaurus rex*, as big as a golf cart. You gaze incredulously at the three-and-a-half-inch eye, which gazes back at you. You measure the six-inch sabers it carries for teeth, and you realize that in real life you would have amounted to nothing more than a gumdrop to this king of consumers. Now a triceratops comes to life. Its eyes flick back and forth, sizing you up. It takes a step forward. There is real menace in its look. Muscles seem to move beneath the skin. The massive body, the grotesque horns, the giant beak, the little, malevolent eye—something clicks in your head, some neural circuit, some ancient racial memory, and for just an instant you are standing in the Cretaceous, seventy million years ago. With a shock you finally comprehend how alien to our mammalian sensibilities the world was, how strange these creatures are, how magnificent, how formidable . . . how extinct.

Then reality presses back. The triceratops moves its head in a series of subtle, mechanical jerks. The valves click. The pistons puff like miniature air brakes. The leg steps back. The eye flicks backward with a knocking sound at the end of the stroke. Before you stands a robot invested in a mannequin.

Superb as it looks, you feel a hollow yearning as you gaze upon it.

You know, and yet deep down something resists the knowledge, that no matter how much paleontology ever translates from the fossil archives, the living touches will never be realized. They are simply not there. And the imagination—well, it is just a dim flicker, confined under the bell jar of what we know of the living. The mind cannot conjure up with any certainty those actions and patterns and sounds of the alien deceased. Who could predict from the ant suspended in amber the social kingdom of its species? Look at the adornments that make a camel a camel, a mandrill a mandrill, a man a man, a woman a woman; for that matter, the mounds of flesh that make a fat man fat. The stuff over the bones leaves not a molecule of evidence behind in the rock. Then you come to the skeleton of *Tyrannosaurus rex*, or *Stegosaurus*, or any ancient creature, and you wonder what fins, what folds, what feathers, what inconceivable ornaments of color and flesh completed the creation. What impulse, what thoughts, what desires must have coursed through its tiny brain? We don't have a clue, nor shall we ever. Dinosaurs will always be creatures of fantasy.

All around you they are bellowing, pawing the earth, raising their heads, moving their tails, taking one step forward, one back. The last factory workers are leaving, however, and the dinosaurs are being turned off for the night. Then an odd thing begins to happen. As the humans go home, leaving you alone in the room, the creatures seem to take on a spiritual life above and beyond their assigned mission as teachers of science and technology. It is as if they want to talk, as if they had secret wisdom on the ironies of evolution, which they are willing to divulge.

Tyrannosaurus fixes its big eye on you. *Allosaurus* glares down. *Stegosaurus* and *Triceratops* gaze in your direction. Robots, you tell yourself. Then comes the first irony. These are indeed monuments to technology—science and technology bent to the illusion of life. But dinosaurs themselves are monuments to extinction. Therefore, dinamations as well are monuments to extinction. You can't think about extinction, however, without thinking about evolution, and dinosaurs bring tablets of stone to the discussion. You look back at *Tyrannosaurus* in wonder. How did such formidable machines of domination ever lose their hold on life? There is no security, saith the mightiest of the tyrants. It is illusion. All things, no matter how mighty, have fatal flaws.

But before they pass they flourish, and before they flourish they find their own path. Ancient evolution makes you aware of the big sweep of things, the broad strokes that made a lineage succeed and, later, fail. Across the room stands *Parasaurolophus*, with its crest of bone that protrudes up and back from its head like a headdress. Apparently it functioned as a horn of bone to magnify its voice, for the air passage travels up through it and doubles back down through the larynx. Nearby stands *Pachycephalosaurus*, its thick, bony helmet of a head an adaptation, probably, for ramming its rivals.

Horns, armor plates, spinal plates, tail spikes, thumb spikes, saber claws, knife teeth, tanklike bodies, gigantism—the sheer physical diversity and range of the dinosaurs has never come close to being equaled by the mammals. But it has by the insects, for the insects, too, developed a range of body sizes and shapes that defies the mind. It's as if evolution were experimenting. With the insect it was solving the problems of life with mechanical devices—spines, spikes, claws, hypodermic mouthparts, spectacular colors and patterns. The insect brain did little more than bring the devices into play. Virtually incapable of all but the dimmest kind of learning, most behavior was hard-wired; the terms "insect" and "instinct" are almost synonyms. And yet the tiny insect brain is capable of inconceivable performance: witness the ants, bees, and termites.

The insects worked out well—so well that evolution apparently thought, "Why not scale them up? Let's see what big, engineered bodies and little, dim brains are capable of doing. We'll call them dinosaurs." So successful were these creatures that they dominated the earth for 160 million years. When extinction finally struck, evolution said, "All right, now that I know what you can do, I'm going to try a new idea."

That new idea was brain power, and the creatures chosen for the experiment were the mammals. It is probably no accident that mammals seem simple in their body design. Evolution is seeing if a big brain in a plain body is more successful in the long run than a little brain in a big, rococo body. The extent of the long run is the key, because one mammal—the one that has built robotic dinosaurs— has succeeded to the point of total world dominion. The only question left is how long it will reign.

Homo sapiens is an odd species, and standing here among the dinamations makes that apparent. We like to think of ourselves as the pinnacle of evolution, but that is too self-congratulating. *Extremity* of evolution is perhaps more accurate. We are off to the side. Way off. All the two-legged dinosaurs had a tail. You think about that as you look at the *Allosaurus* standing before you. In fact, all other bipeds had or have tails. We are the only ones that don't; in fact, our first act as a lineage was to dispose of our tails. That means we must have had extremely powerful brains from the start. Standing fully upright is like balancing a pencil on its point, and it can be accomplished only by using an extremely sophisticated computer which integrates balance and muscular coordination. What tail-balanced biped has a program so sophisticated that it can breakdance, ice skate, walk the high wire and the balance beam, sprint for a bus, lug out the trash, or kick an opponent in the shins? The human brain is a clever replacement for the tail.

If you look at it from an evolutionary point of view, the human brain is just a different kind of gigantism. If you could take our minds—the sum of our feelings, thoughts, impulses—and cast them in physical form, you would gaze upon a collection of sizes and shapes that would make the dinosaurs positively boring. Einsteins, Ted Bundys, Newtons, Hitlers, Mozarts, Shakespeares, popes, and saints—the range exceeds comprehension. It's sobering to think that gigantism goeth before a fall.

The time has come to exit the building. The lights flick off, and the saurian robots hulk in the darkness. Or maybe it is not darkness, but the past. They have been dead these past 70,001,990 years—ever since the Cretaceous period ended at 2:12 P.M. on March 2, seventy million B.C. I give the "exact time" to illustrate how ludicrously short and preposterously self-centered our human concept of time is. When you deal with environmental impact and ecological change, you must think in earth time the rate at which the planet ages and changes naturally.

To put us in perspective, let us go forward seventy million years and see what the fossil record has to say about *Homo sapiens*. Straightaway we run into a curious problem: the smallest increment the fossil record can resolve is about one hundred thousand years; anything that happens closer together than one hundred thousand years can't be separated. This means we would be hard-pressed to tell from the fossil record whether Christ came before or after the computer—or even, for that matter, whether he came before Neanderthal man, or whether Neanderthal man came after the nuclear age, which would make a lot of sense.

The point is, human civilization has arisen so fast in comparison to the rhythms of the natural world that it cannot be measured in geological time. It is like a subatomic flash. An alien race arriving in seventy million years would conclude that we had arrived instantly, perhaps from another planet. The critical question is, how do you control a flash? A greenhouse effect caused in the last hundred years, a hole in the ozone layer in the past thirty years; three billion people added to the population since 1950—the rapidity of these trends is out of all proportion with ecological/geological change, and we are currently engaged in one of the planet's greatest and fastest extinctions. It will be indistinguishable from the impact of an asteroid. We are, in other words, the instrument of extinction.

So the dinamations are going far beyond their assigned task of teaching the enjoyment of science and technology. They are playing philosophic hardball and asking the ultimate questions. Is the human mind any more capable of controlling its destiny than those great lumbering creatures whose effigies lurk behind the workshop doors? Is science the answer, or is it merely blind intellectual gigantism?

As you leave the Dinamation plant and walk out to your car, you join the countless millions of your species in a living tribute to evolution and extinction and technology. You reach for the ignition, turn the key, and the engine leaps to life. Gasoline courses through its veins. Gasoline, a liquid extracted from the bodies of the dinosaurs. Industrial civilization, a gigantic monument to extinction.

PICTURES

||————————————————————————————||

AT A

||————————————————————————————||

SCIENTIFIC

||————————————————————————————||

EXHIBITION

The first day of classes, fall semester 1964. Twelve of us are gathered in the physiology laboratory. Twelve twenty- and twenty-one-year-olds with our translucent skin, shiny hair, clear eyes, virgin minds (which is to say, empty and unformed). Fluorescent boxes in the ceiling irradiate the room with a cold, hard light as we sit on stools around the black-slab laboratory tables discreetly assessing one another. Our hair is neatly trimmed and combed (men) or permed and cut at shoulder length (women). The men wear plain cotton slacks and short-sleeved shirts, the women wear calf-length skirts or jeans and long-sleeved blouses. New notebooks lie open on the lab bench before us, notebooks fresh from the bookstore and as yet unblemished by the doodled graffiti of lectures endured.

We have assembled for that ritual of higher education in which the young throw back their heads, drop their lower jaws onto their chests, and allow the priests of knowledge to stuff concepts, facts, and attitudes into the vacant spaces.

To the outside world we are carefree youth, but within our college society we are miserable with the anxieties of scholarship. How much work will the course require, how tough will our competition be? To the outside world we are thirsty for knowledge, but inwardly we are already thinking about the final grade. That is our goal, not knowledge. Knowledge is merely a by-product of the study needed for acquiring a good grade, for without good grades we will not be admitted to medical school or graduate studies.

The teaching assistant enters the room pushing a stainless steel lab cart. On top of it sit several plastic containers like vegetable crispers, with small, screened windows cut in the sides. Squeaks and squeals emanate from within, as does the odor of rat culture. We are all familiar with the teaching assistant from other courses we have taken. He is a Ph.D. candidate and is known informally as Owl. He has a very round head; round horn-rimmed glasses; a soft, muffled voice; and a peculiar manner of staring without blinking, with no outward sign of emotion. He parks his cartful of rats next to the laboratory sink with its straight, black, concrete sides, turns, and gazes at us. Just gazes and gazes.

Now the professor enters. He is a tall, gaunt young man with a long, narrow face, pale gray eyes, and short gray-blond hair. This is his first university post, and he has been assigned the task of introducing us to the science of physiology.

Exercise No. 1. Come and gather around today's laboratory apparatus, he says, and he begins to explain what this first class is about. This is a photospectrometer, he declares, a word which emerges from his mouth in chunks and rivals a standard American sentence in length. He lays his hand on a large, boxy machine the size of a filing cabinet, with lights and gauges on its front panel.

We are going to demonstrate the action of liver enzymes. We are going to mix them with a substrate (a substance for the enzyme molecules to chew on), and the mixture will start out with a dark blue color. When the reaction occurs, the color will change, and we will measure this change with the photospectrometer.

It is not easy to run a good experiment, the professor informs us. It must be designed correctly. It needs to have a control, an identical experiment run at the same time in which the variable in question is not tested—in other words, a blank run. This gives a baseline against which the experimental treatments can be compared. We will run one test with only the blue substrate in the test tube—no enzymes added. To the others we will add the liver extract.

A good experiment has also to be made statistically sound. It must be repeated a number of times to make sure the results are not fluke occurrences. It must be analyzed and interpreted properly. If the findings are solid and firm, the experiment can then be repeated by others in other places and it will give the same results. Experimentation is the basis of scientific progress, and we will be sent into the future well trained in the theory, the basic methodology, and the proper psychology of research.

Now for the rats. They are here to provide us with livers. It's somewhat of a nuisance, really, because the liver cases—that is, the rats themselves—must be opened up in order to get the liver out. But this is part of science. Here is how we take out livers.

Owl steps forward to demonstrate. He lifts the lid from one of the containers and motions us to gather around. Four or five rats rise up on their hind legs to look out at us. Their whiskers twitch; their little black eyes twinkle and glint in the fluorescent lighting of the laboratory. This is the first time they have seen this new environment, so they are curious. They stand with their paws clinging to the edge and look up. They drop to all fours and proceed nervously around the perimeter of their container. They push their noses into the corners, then up to the top of the walls. They rise up on their haunches, lick their fur, and stand up against the side of the box to smell the air, straining in their dim minds to make sense of it all. They are exercising the rudiments of that glorious exaggeration which we humans call scientific curiosity.

Okay, says Owl, you do it like this. He reaches in and grabs the tail of a strapping big male with black-and-white blotches over its body. He walks over to the sink holding the rat by its tail, its head and neck straining to look up at us, its legs splayed out stiffly, groping for something to hold. You whirl it three times, says Owl, and on the third time, you smash its head against the sink like this. *Shmeck.* The sound of smashing cartilage and splintering bone.

The body goes stiff. Its legs reach out in a futile grasp for its fading life. Then it stiffens in a final convulsion. Feces erupt from the anus, and urine squirts from the penis, followed by semen. It's as if the creature has jettisoned everything in a desperate, valiant attempt to evade death. A few of the students wince.

All right, says the professor. I want you to pair off in teams. I want each team to kill its own rats. It's good experience. Some of the students are not enthralled with this prospect, but each team manages to elect an executioner. These are the partners who, even if they balk at the task, will still force themselves to do what has to be done for a higher cause, which in this case, is the course grade.

The rats look up. We students look down. We have shared ancestry with these creatures—we had the same brain, the same mind, until some sixty-eight million years ago, when our destinies split. Having scaled the tree of evolution, swelling, refining, convoluting, that once-shared brain has now returned to operate on its source.

The quest for livers begins. It quickly becomes clear that the task will not be as easy as Owl has made it appear. These are large animals, a pound or more. They have extremely large teeth, which they nervously and loudly grind and sharpen. It's not so easy to catch them by the tail; as a hand approaches they turn and face it with what looks like malice.

We persevere, and, holding rats, several of us approach the sink.

We move tentatively. How hard do you swing? Is it easy to hit the sink with the head? The first tentative *shmeck* slaps across the room. The rat is only crippled. The student, a petite blonde, gasps and drops the dazed creature. It gnashes its teeth and tries to run, but its right side is crippled and it spins in circles, smearing urine over the pale green linoleum and leaving a trail of fecal pellets. Another tentative *shmeck*. Another crippled rat writhing and convulsing on the floor, trying to bite the foot of its assailant. People dance along with the rat. Owl steps in and expertly grabs the tail of one, whirls it three times, smashes its skull on the granite sink. He grabs the second rat, and repeats the maneuver, but this time with only one deft whirl.

The students look down, look away; some hide their faces with their hands. Neither the professor nor Owl says anything about empathy or the ethics of killing in the name of science, to say nothing of the spiritual price of killing in the first place. It is assumed that students of biology have resolved these issues by the time they reach their junior year of university.

Owl now places the big black-and-white rat on the lab bench and with a scalpel cuts up the midline of the belly. Pulling the skin and fur aside, he then cuts through the sheet of stomach muscle, exposing the inner workings. Large and small intestines lie efficiently coiled and packed behind the liver, which covers the heart. Reaching in, Owl pushes the other organs aside, separates the lobes of the liver, and cuts the purple-brown tissue free. He shoves the rest of the viscera, whose cells have not yet died, back into the carcass, steps on the pedal of the trash canister, popping up the lid, and dumps the carcass into the black metallic void. The dead animal has no further use. It will be tossed into the dumpster behind the life sciences building and, along with other refuse, will eventually find its way into the municipal dump.

Turning to the object of the exercise, Owl drops the liver into a Waring blender, pours in several additives, and turns the machine on. Within seconds, a frothy red liquid like a raspberry milkshake is ready for the test tubes. The rest of us follow his example. Soon a statistically satisfying battery of identical experiments are cooking away atop the black laboratory benches. Several hours later, notebooks safely pressing the data against opposing pages, we are walking home with our first lesson completed.

Exercise No. 2. Today we will study the heart of the turtle. Like all muscle, it operates by passing the ions of calcium, potassium, and sodium through its membranes. If you bathe the heart in different concentrations of these various substances, the heartbeat will speed up, slow down, go into tetanic contraction, or simply stop beating for lack of proper ionic balance. Today's exercise will demonstrate this amazing gimmick of physiology using freshwater turtles, which Owl will demonstrate how to open.

He reaches into a large bucket and picks a specimen out. From above, it is a brownish, mottled oval about ten inches long. It is much flatter than a land-dwelling tortoise, and a series of plates meet in the middle of the shell, forming a rooftop ridge which follows the contour of the carapace. The legs are folded neatly into crevices at the four corners of the shell, the tail is pressed tensely across the rear, and the head is retracted completely out of sight beneath the carapace overhang.

With his free hand Owl picks up a stainless steel probe with a blunt hook at the end. He pokes this into the sanctuary between the front legs, fishes about, and catches something. He pulls harder and draws forth the turtle's head, which he has hooked beneath the chin. He continues to pull until the neck is fully extended. It is dark green and streaked from front to back with alternating black and yellow stripes.

Here, says Owl, and motions for the president of the local fraternity, a tall, slender youth with a friendly smile and kindly eyes, to assume command of the turtle. His job will be to keep the neck drawn out. Picking up a massive pair of electrician's pliers, Owl informs us that what he is doing is called "pithing." He takes the pliers and squeezes down on the turtle's extended neck. Crunch, crunch, crunch. With the bone of the vertebrae collapsing, the nerves of the spinal cord compressing into mush, Owl works the pliers methodically, from behind the head along the entire four-inch length to the neck's base. The four legs pop from their crevices and lash wildly—they have been freed from the central government of the brain. In fact, the purpose of pithing is to cut off the neuronal commands from the brain. Any action the heart produces will therefore be generated by the heart muscle itself. Signals from central command, the turtle's brain, will thus be unable to confound the issue. Meanwhile, the head dangles on the end of the mangled neck, the brain still alive, its natural thoughts never again to reach the body.

Now, says Owl, this is how you get to the heart. He picks up a hacksaw.

Hold the turtle like this, he says to the fraternity president, who grimaces. Owl takes the living corpse and shows how to hold the thing on its back, firmly. He lays the hacksaw along the left margin of the plastron (the turtle's stomach plate) and begins to saw.

Little beads of scientific sweat appear on Owl's furrowed brow as he pulls and pushes the blade across the turtle's shell. The teeth make a slippery hissing sound as they cut into the living tissue, into the epithelial cells covering the bone, into the living osteoblastic tissue itself; a slimy paste of finely ground bone, skin, and blood builds up in a wad at each end of the cut.

Thunk. The saw cuts through, into the body cavity. Owl rotates the turtle and commences to saw through the right margin of the plastron. Thunk. The other side is severed, and the plastron now floats on the soft, tightly packed viscera. Owl grasps it and lifts. But membranes as clear as plastic wrap still bind the plastron to the body. Blood vessels, still throbbing with the beat of the nearby heart, are suspended in the membranous plane. Owl cuts through it all with a scalpel. He tosses the plastron into the metal refuse can.

For no particular reason, a thought strikes at this point (the thought would be just as apt while the neck is being crushed): *This was a living, sentient creature. To mutilate it without any anesthesia, to dissect and manipulate its still-living corpse with cold detachment, is . . . ghastly.* A shiver runs across the shoulders and down the spine. But it is a fleeting reflex. There is no time to indulge in reveries here. Owl is explaining the preparation of the heart.

It is a tricky, delicate operation, but Owl works with sure fingers. Before long, blood vessels have been cut and the heart has been attached to a long lever which pivots at its center. A string runs from a hook embedded in the turtle's ventricle to one end of the lever. The other end holds an ink pen. As the heart contracts and relaxes, the lever rises and falls, trailing the pen over a rotating cylinder. Graph paper is wrapped around the cylinder, so as the lever rises and falls it records the heart's performance. The device is called a kymograph.

It is now our turn to crush the necks of our own turtles and repeat the preparation of a turtle's heart. The reaction of the students, female as well as male, is not so noticeable as it was when we were killing and dissecting rats several weeks earlier.

Soon eight more turtle heads are drawn forth from their shells; eight more brains are made into living pendulums on the ends of crushed necks, counting off the last moments of consciousness; and eight more plastrons are being sawed through. All that remains now is to bathe the hearts in various solutions so that we can see for ourselves that muscle does indeed obey chemical-mechanical laws, laws just as mechanistic as the levers that the heart is pulling up and down.

Exercise No. 3. This promises to be a light day's work. We are testing the ability of hemoglobin and other respiratory pigments to carry oxygen. More miniature oil refineries have been set on the lab bench. The hemoglobin has been purchased from a biological supply house, so there is nothing to dismember or kill. Except for a bowl filled with a writhing pasta of polychaete marine worms from the genus *Glycera*. They contain a kind of hemoglobin, which we will test for its oxygen-carrying capacity, time permitting.

These are interesting creatures, the professor tells us, because of their hydraulic jaws. It seems that they possess in their throats a hollow, extensible tube, on the end of which grow four long, sharp, poisonous fangs, for *Glycera* is a predator. When it strikes it contracts the muscles of its body wall, forcing fluid into the proboscis and forcing the proboscis out through the mouth into the environment. As the tip of this long, tonguelike organ nears the end of its strike, the four teeth open in a ready-to-grab position; when the muscles relax, the proboscis starts to retract and the teeth close down, grabbing the quarry.

This description arouses some curiosity, and during a lull in the proceedings, laughing and animated chatter come from one corner of the room. Several of the male students are watching another perform some sort of manipulation in a petri dish. A husky blond lad with crewcut hair and horn-rimmed glasses is wielding a very large syringe. A closer look shows what he is doing: He is injecting water into a *Glycera* worm, and he is grinning gleefully.

The powerless creature is so fully inflated that it cannot move, cannot even writhe, and its proboscis is now a long turgid nipple protruding from the front. It looks like a water-filled condom, except for the teeth. It is hard to feel much empathy for such a worm, and besides, we are growing accustomed to the scientific use of life. There is something humorous in the worm's bloated plight. Ha ha. The prankster, now laughing, withdraws the syringe from the worm. But before he can react, a thin stream of water squirts from the syringe wound, almost as if the worm is consciously shooting back, and sprays all over the student's spectacles, face, and shirt. This is really funny. Ha ha ha.

Exercise No. 4. Today's chore will be to measure the insulating effect of fur. We will use mice.

The basic procedure is quite simple, says the instructor. We will measure how fast a mouse consumes oxygen at room temperature, at 15°C, and at 5°C. Then we will shave half of its body and see how quickly it burns oxygen while half-naked at each of the same three temperatures. Finally, we will shave the rest of the mouse and repeat the measurements again. Everyone knows that the mice will have to burn more oxygen; common sense tells us that a fur coat retains warmth. But this procedure will allow us to measure how efficiently the warmth is retained; it will measure, quantify, assign hard numbers to the effect. Now, after months of preparations, dissections, and demonstrations, we are quite used to the sacrifice of life. This exercise will not even require us to kill the mice. We will merely have to shave the specimens and take their temperature. The temperature is important to know because when the mouse cannot produce enough heat to offset the cold, its internal temperature will drop and there will be no need to continue the cold treatment; to continue would simply be to waste our valuable time.

Owl demonstrates the proper grip for taking a rectal temperature. With his left hand he plucks a mouse from its container and grips the head. He places his index finger under the mouse's throat, his thumb on the back of its neck. The mouse's body lies across the palm of his hand, the tail lashing and the legs straining against Owl's palm. Owl picks up a small thermometer with a bulb the diameter of a heavy pencil lead. It is tiny by human standards, but by mouse dimensions it is roughly the equivalent of a police baton. Owl prepares to push it up the little rodent's anus.

As the monumental event proceeds, the mouse urinates, of course. We have come to expect these excretory reactions from our subjects. After all, to a mouse or a rat the experience is probably similar to an encounter with King Kong. The titanic ape's coordination probably is not too fine and his baton technique is not very gentle, and, maybe, it causes excruciating pain. Anyhow, Owl's demonstration gives meaning to the term "manhandle."

We have come to class equipped with heavy ski coats, because the experiment requires us to sit with the mice in the cold-storage rooms for forty-five minutes at a stretch. The mouse sits in an airtight container containing a respirometer, a device that measures the amount of oxygen used and the carbon dioxide produced. During the first run with fully furred specimens, the mice merely settle down in a tight, hunched-up position and shiver. We shiver too, and *we* are wearing winter clothes.

Now comes the exercise in shaving. Owl provides us with manual hair clippers designed for home use on humans. These are large and clumsy devices and the mice end up nicked and bloodied. (The nick from a barber's shears scales up, on a mouse, to a two-foot wound on a human body.)

Back in the cold rooms, the mice hunch and shiver violently. The rear halves of their bodies are raggedly shorn, like absurd miniature parodies of poodles. They squeeze their eyes shut. A dog, which is a social animal and can expect to attract attention and even care, would whine in such a situation, but a mouse is not a social creature and its instincts have not been crafted to respond with supplications for aid. They endure the cold silently. Forty-five minutes later we return to the lab to complete the job of shaving the mice.

We learn at this point that some of the students have had trouble with the temperature readings. Female mice have a large pad of flesh, which includes the anus and the vaginal openings. The anus is not easy to pick out in this pink bed of skin, especially the first time you work with mice, and Ray, a big, affable football player with an Elvis Presley haircut, is having difficulties nearby. He holds a bedraggled and groggy little female between a beefy index finger and a thumb, which is larger than the mouse itself. Its anal pad is bloody, and it kicks and evacuates desperately. Heh, heh, says Ray with a sheepish grin, I think I just synthesized an anus. The thermometers are sharp. In the hands of such a human, they can easily penetrate the flesh. The mouse will die of its wounds.

Suddenly the quiet murmur of students shaving mice and taking their temperatures is interrupted by a string of words that sock like fists into our rapt, laboratory concentration.

SHIT. FUCK. PISS. CRAP.

These admonitions emerge at measured intervals from the mouth of Owl. Fury is escaping from his ruptured calm like steam and everyone whirls around, mice, clippers, and thermometers in hand. There stands our teaching assistant. He holds his right arm at a stiff ninety-degree angle from his body, like a German salute, and dangling from the end of his middle finger is a mouse with little shaved buttocks. Its teeth are embedded in the finger pad. It is doing its very best to accommodate Owl's commands.

The final test, with naked mice, proceeds without a hitch. Most of the mice reach their metabolic limits, and their body temperatures begin to plummet, which cuts the experiment short. We will get to go home a few minutes earlier than expected. What remains is to analyze our data and write our findings in proper scientific format.

The course ends. We write our reports and get our grades. We haven't learned anything new to science. For the most part these exercises have merely repeated the experiments of an earlier time. They were nothing more than training exercises in which we used living creatures as educational sacrifices. What we have learned, aside from the basics of experimental methodology, are two lessons that are fundamental to Western biological science. First, we have learned to distance ourselves from feeling, to dissect intellect and separate it from emotion. In other words, we have become calloused. We can take the lives of little creatures and dismember their bodies with barely a twinge of empathy, compassion, guilt, or remorse. Second, and most fundamental, we have acquired a scientific system of values. We have learned that animals deemed appropriate for experimentation have no value at all. That is why their lives can be so blithely discarded.

Fall 1988. Twenty-four years have passed since the physiology class. Most of us have gone on to our distinguished careers. The fraternity president, the demure blonde, Ray the football player, and several others have all become medical doctors. The instructor has become the chairman of his department. Owl has become the chairman of the biology department at another university. The injector of worms is writing this essay. We learned our lessons well.

In the past five or six years animal rights has become a significant issue, and it has forced some improvements in the treatment of experimental animals. These mainly involve humane, sanitary maintenance. The basic attitude toward scientific use of animals has not changed, however. Fifteen years ago I saw several of my peers close down their laboratory for the evening, and as they cleaned up after the day's experimentation they found that three or four mice were left over. The next experiments were not scheduled for several weeeks, and it wasn't worth the cost and effort to keep the mice alive until then. My friends simply threw the extras into a blender, ground them up, and washed them down the sink. This was called the Bloody Mary solution. Several days ago I talked with another old peer from my university days, and she informs me that the new, humane method for discarding extra mice in her lab is to seal them in a plastic bag and put it in the freezer.

I repeat: the attitude toward nonhuman life has not changed among experimental biologists. Attitude is merely a projection of one's values, and their values have not changed; they do not respect life that is not human.

This is not to say that scientists who use the lives of animals are bad people. They are products of their culture. Their values and attitudes are practical and functional and suited to the job of doing modern biological science. You cannot pursue science if you place animal and human lives on planes of equal altitude. You cannot pursue medicine, especially the surgical branches, if you cannot harden your reactions to cutting the flesh of living patients. No matter how agonizing the act may be, you must do what scientific thought prescribes. Science and medicine require the intellect to lead the way.

I submit that by certifying these values, we have put ourselves in a serious bind.

The problem is this. Most human beings are, I believe, born with the rudiments of compassion and empathy, guilt and remorse (the guilt and the remorse reinforce the empathy and compassion). Through proper training and nurture, these emotional virtues become the foundation of humanity. However, the training for experimental biology—and, generally, for all of science and technology—starves these undeveloped qualities. The fact is, one fundamental purpose of scientific training is to separate rational thought from emotion, which is thought to distort the operation of reason. The question then arises: once we have molded our scientists to think in a mode without feeling, why should they shift values when they come to questions of human life? To put it another way, what is the risk of scientific training, of acquiring scientific values? The answer has to lie in the nature of intellect itself.

Science deals with the physical world, as opposed to the spiritual. Science asks how the world works; it looks for the laws of physical reality. When we attach the hearts of turtles to the kymograph, we are examining the physiological action of ions and hormones on heart muscle. Pour in one solution, and the heart speeds up. Pour in another, and it stops beating. The lever bounces up and down with the pulsing of the heart, or holds flat and motionless when the pulsations cease. When we measure the temperatures and metabolic rates of mice with fur, mice with semishaved bodies, and mice naked and semicomatose with cold, we are gathering data; we analyze it, convert it to graphs with rounded peaks and valleys, and convert it further to equations and mathematical formulae. What goes on in our minds? I will tell you: pleasure in getting good data, a sense of accomplishment from a hard exercise completed, perhaps an aesthetic satisfaction in the graphic forms. The abstract, intellectual beauty of biological laws.

The truth is, the reasoning process is just as mechanistic as levers themselves. It is a system of mental levers and gears. Its purpose is to track and capture the mechanical laws that make the physical world work, and it reflects its purpose. In its pure state, reason has no feelings, no warmth, no compassion or empathy, no remorse or guilt. Reason has no more soul than the computer, than the electronic text and graphs and animated forms that flash across a screen.

Reason leads to factual knowledge, not to wisdom; wisdom is much bigger and far more complex than scientific comprehension. Wisdom sweeps across all the realms of human experience, across religion, ethics, philosophy, aesthetics, knowledge; it is the ultimate human attainment. Scientific reason, scientific knowledge, should never be accorded more than servant status in the house of wisdom.

What happens when people of science are left to the guidance of their rational minds? Well, the great majority seem to remain in touch with humanity, restricting their mechanistic values to their fields of expertise. That testifies to an innate decency of the human majority. However, I do not think we recognize how easy it is for reason to get off track. And when it does go wrong, when it does get beyond wisdom, may heaven help us.

Let us consider a recently publicized example of science gone bad. During the Second World War, a scientist named Dr. Sigmund Rascher ran a series of four hundred experiments on the effects of exposure to cold. Dr. Rascher did his work at Dachau concentration camp, and he chose as his experimental subjects some three hundred Gypsies, Jews, Poles, and Russians. The U.S. Army recovered extensive research records, which included accounts of materials and methods, charts, graphs, and descriptions.

One of Dr. Rascher's research goals was to discover how long the human being could survive in cold water. In pursuit of this knowl-

edge, he immersed his subjects in vats of water at temperatures between 36°F and 53°F. He and his assistants took temperatures as if
they were using mice. They recorded every reaction in minute detail: They described the vomiting, the foaming at the mouth, the
agonized bellowing; the measured changes in the blood, in the urine, in the spinal fluid, in muscle reflex, in the action of the heart.

Usually we dismiss German war atrocities as pure torture, nothing more. But one fact punctures that assumption: Torturers do not
record their results, certainly not with scientific accuracy and precision. Nor do they go through the sophisticated cogitations of casting torture in the form of correct experimental method. Scientists
design experiments, then they record results, meticulously. It is difficult, demanding work.

It is impossible to know what went on in the minds of Dr. Rascher
and his colleagues. They were torturers, without question. Un-
doubtedly they embraced the anti-Semitic and Aryan notions of
Hitler's Reich. They probably felt confident that Germany would
win the war and they would be unaccountable. But, at least in the
case of cold exposure, they also saw themselves as scientists, as in-
vestigators pursuing scientific knowledge and recording the work
for others to scrutinize.

It turns out that the experiments on cold exposure were indeed
motivated by practical considerations. German pilots shot down
over the ocean were dying of exposure, and German soldiers were
freezing on the Russian front. The military wanted to save its men.
And so a group of medical doctors associated with the Luftwaffe and
the Air Ministry, professionals who were highly respected and superior in rank, developed the basic research goals and supervised Dr.
Rascher's activities. Scientific intellect and the torturer's art had
met and fused in the pursuit of knowledge.

With these dearly purchased data the Dachau doctors developed
what was considered for many years the most effective treatment for
cold exposure. Major Leo Alexander, an army doctor and medical

investigator for the U.S. secretary of war, reviewed Rascher's work, and his conclusions are quoted in an article in the *Los Angeles Times* (10/30/88). As Dr. Alexander put it, "Dr. Rascher, although he wallowed in blood . . . and in obscenity . . . nevertheless appears to have settled the question of what to do for people in shock from exposure to cold. . . . The method of rapid and intensive rewarming in hot water . . . should be immediately adopted as the treatment of choice by the Air Sea Rescue Services of the United States Armed Forces."

We presume that we live in an enlightened age. Television, newspapers, and books advocate undying vigilance to prevent a repetition of the Holocaust. Yet while we all look for the threat in the political realm, I have the uneasy feeling that we are looking the wrong way. The demon lives deeper than politics or nationality. It lives in the human mind. The demon is reason.

In its pursuit of knowledge, this mechanistic part of the mind turns whichever way the questions call. And do not assume that only Nazis are capable of scientific atrocities. I have seen documentary film footage in which disciples of Ivan Petrovich Pavlov experimented with human subjects, using orphans to test the conditioned response. These researchers strapped the terrified subjects into massive chairs, cut holes through the children's cheeks, and glued glass tubes into the opening to catch and measure the saliva dripping from the end.

Nor are American doctors and scientists above the darker temptations of scientific reason. The Central Intelligence Agency is known to have tested pathologic microbes on the people of San Francisco and New York. The U.S. Public Health Service followed the progress of syphilis in four hundred Alabama black men for a period of forty years, 1932–1972. Penicillin was available from the late 1940s, but the doctors wanted to know how syphilis proceeds and so refrained from treating their subjects. From the mid-1950s to the early 1970s a research team from New York University inoculated with hepatitis virus a group of severely retarded children at the Willowbrook State School—again, to follow the course of development and to seek a cure. A doctor named Henry Beecher compiled a list of more than fifty of these and similar experiments in 1966; he pointed out that the list was not nearly comprehensive.

That is what happens when scientific intellect sneaks over the walls of empathy, compassion, reverence, love—when it gets past the humane emotions.

But reason in general is a most insidious thing. The purpose of a brain is to help its body survive; the purpose of reason is therefore to serve its own interests. I am convinced that one of the main functions of the rational mind is to deceive itself, for the simple and compelling reason that people fight hardest, and have the best chances of gaining their ends, when they believe that their cause is right, good, proper. In other words, *Homo sapiens* is not a rational animal: It is a rational*izing* one. Human experimentation is always done for some high *reason*—to save the country, to better the human condition, to advance the state of medicine, to preserve the superrace. And on and on.

And so even in this age of scientific light we practice experiments on animals that on humans are atrocities. On animals they are considered standard research methods. Reason has convinced most of us that it is morally defensible to sacrifice, dismember, drug, and otherwise manipulate animals in the pursuit of scientific knowledge. Only when the same methods are applied to humans do we bother to look behind the rationalizations and realize how abominable, painful, and cruel our science can be.

I am very aware of the power and the glory of scientific thought; I am, after all, a scientist by training. Science and technology are the foundations of modern civilization. (Never mind that they are also the cause of global decay and that the only guaranteed cure of an ailment is to eliminate the cause—that is another story.) Furthermore, the human being has no choice but to follow its conscious intellect; reasoned thought is a fundamental activity in our natural history. We cannot *not* do research.

But I am also acutely aware that reason, as well as being wonderful, is terrible in its power. Indeed, I've seen that power start to swell on the first day of class, when the instructor begins teaching his values and attitudes toward other forms of life.

What can be done? Why not begin on that first day of biology to explain the dark side of the reasoning intellect? Make us realize that the goals of science—those cold, shiny, indestructible grains of fact, those intricate, glinting, mechanical contrivances of theory—carry a price tag. The price is humanity. Each sacrifice, each dissection, each surgical incision is drawn on the account of good and decency. Explain that if the scientific mind does escape its cage of empathy, compassion, respect, reverence, humility, and gratitude, the ultimate price is human life, because to the scientific intellect, the supreme experimental animal is *Homo sapiens*.

Go on to emphasize, during those courses on biology, ways to realign our feelings with our intellect, ways to slow down and reflect on what we are about to do, on the finality of the acts we are about to commit, the pain we are about to inflict, the incomprehensible miracle of organized matter that we are about to destroy when we perform scientific experiments. Take time before each session to consider things from the animal's point of view. Imagine the needle penetrating the stomach muscles, the thermometer being forced up the anus, pliers crushing the vertebrae of the neck. Mention the intimate kinship of all life on earth, as compared to the simple, frozen molecules that constitute the empty universe we have found. Then teach some small gesture, some little expression of thanks to the creature for the gift of its body and its life, which it is about to give. Say a small prayer for its soul. Say a small prayer for the souls of us all.

Design by David Bullen
Typeset in Mergenthaler Goudy Olde Style
with Pegasus display
by Wilsted & Taylor
Printed by Maple-Vail
on acid-free paper